Iguana Invasion!

Iguana Invasion!

Exotic Pets Gone Wild in Florida

Virginia Aronson
and
Allyn Szejko

Pineapple Press, Inc.
Sarasota, Florida

Inquiries should be addressed to:

Pineapple Press, Inc.
P.O. Box 3889
Sarasota, Florida 34230

www.pineapplepress.com

Library of Congress Cataloging-in-Publication Data

Aronson, Virginia.
  Iguana invasion! : exotic pets gone wild in Florida / Virginia Aronson and Allyn Szejko. -- 1st ed.
    p. cm.
  Includes bibliographical references and index.
  ISBN 978-1-56164-468-1 (hb : alk. paper) -- ISBN 978-1-56164-469-8 (pb : alk. paper)
  1. Iguanas as pets--Florida--Juvenile literature. 2. Iguana (Genus)--Florida--Juvenile literature. I. Szejko, Allyn. II. Title.
  SF459.I38A76 2009
  639.3'909759--dc22
                                        2009042152

First Edition
10 9 8 7 6 5 4 3 2 1

Design by Jennifer Borresen
Printed in China

Contents

Introduction

by Allyn Szejko

I am a licensed humane trapper and wildlife rehabilitator. My job is to help wild animals and the people who need my help with them. This can be a thrilling and scary, fun and exhausting job, and I love it.

I guess I've always been an animal lover. When I was in elementary school, I rescued stray dogs and cats around my upstate New York neighborhood. Sometimes I would bring them home for some tender loving care. Living down the street was a man who trapped wild animals and skinned them. This upset me. He hung the animal skins outside his house, probably to dry in the sun. Whenever I walked past his yard I felt frightened and a little sick.

One day my father hired the trapper to catch a woodchuck that was chewing on garbage bins, cardboard boxes, and other juicy morsels in our garage. The trapper set out his "bear trap." It was a metal leghold trap like you see in cartoons, with jagged teeth that can clamp tight on an animal's leg. Later that day, the curious woodchuck stuck his furry head in the trap. It sprung, snapping shut on his little face!

As soon as I heard the poor thing screeching, I ran to the trapper for help. I expected him to release the woodchuck. I wanted to nurse it back to health. Instead, the trapper killed the woodchuck quickly and took it away. I felt heartsick.

Now I work as a wildlife trapper myself. But I am licensed as a humane trapper and wildlife rehabilitator. This means I do not trap animals in ways that hurt them. I use a simple net with a long handle called a "monkey net." I also use a rope made into a noose on a long pole. This is called a "catch pole."

After I gently snare a wild animal in my net or noose, I'll carefully place it in a portable cage. Then I can carry it in my van. I will either return the animal to its natural habitat or bring it to a local wildlife center. Whenever I am called to rescue an injured animal, I will help it as much as I can before I rush it to a wildlife rehabilitation center. There it can get full medical care.

Sometimes an animal has been hit by a car or otherwise seriously injured. If it is in great pain and cannot be treated, I must "euthanize" the suffering animal. To euthanize an animal is to end its life. Sometimes this is for the best.

Occasionally, I will bring an injured animal back to my house to treat it. Once it is healthy again, I release the animal in its natural habitat.

But when an animal I rescue is not native to the state of Florida, it is against the law for me to release it. This means I cannot return such animals to the places where I rescued them. And I cannot turn them loose in the Everglades or other wild areas. Instead, I must find a home for any non-native or "exotic" animal I rescue.

When I first moved to Florida in the 1970s, it was easy to find a loving home for the occasional out-of-place, non-native animal. Now times have changed, and so has our wildlife. These days, we have more than 200 species of exotic animals living in Florida!

Most of these animals were once pets, or are the offspring of former pets. Once the non-native animals escape or are set free by their owners, many of them find Florida to be a great place to live.

After all, it is warm here and the winters are mild. There is plenty to eat because it is so sunny and rainy. In fact, we have more kinds of trees growing here than in any other U.S.

state! Many varieties of non-native plants thrive in Florida too. All this greenery attracts insects, birds, and other animals, both native and exotic. There are flowers and blooms, fruits and shoots all year long. I work in south Florida. Here, many species of exotic animals can live outdoors quite comfortably year-round.

With all this food and sunshine, the non-native animals can breed. And since the seasons are not as distinct as they are farther north, sometimes the animals will breed throughout the year. And then their offspring will breed too. Suddenly, there's a population explosion of non-native species!

Non-Natives, Exotics, and Invasives

Just what is a non-native or exotic species? In Florida, it is defined by two things:

- ▪ it ranges freely;
- ▪ it was not native here in the time before Christopher Columbus arrived in America.

Non-native animals come from a foreign environment. Some were brought to Florida for sale as pets. Others were stowaways on ships from other countries. We have a dozen international ports in this state. We import many items from all over the world. Sometimes lizards, frogs, snakes, and other animals are on the ships that come to our ports. From there, they escape and find themselves a new home.

Iguanas soak up sun to keep their bodies warm.

In our state, invasive animals are non-native ones that are destructive to Florida. Invasives cause harm by competing with our native animals. Invasives take native species' food and nests. They take over other animals' territories. Invasives might even eat our native animals. Invasives may alter Florida's ecosystem and create unhealthy imbalances. Animals evolve over time to be better able to live in their environment. Invasive animals did not evolve in the environment they have invaded. So how can they live there? The answer is that no predators have evolved to hold them back. Predators are nature's way of keeping species in balance. Without predators, animal populations can grow too big and too quickly.

The most serious threat to animals is loss of habitat, usually because humans move in. The second most serious threat is invasion by foreign species. Invasive species actually do very well sharing their habitat with humans. They adapt easily to new situations. Invasive species are a particular problem on islands. Getting rid of these invasive species is expensive, and usually impossible.

Florida Exotics

In Florida, we face a growing problem of exotic animal species on the loose. This is why I am not surprised anymore when I get calls from policemen who need help capturing 12-foot pythons. I'm also not surprised to hear from frightened elderly women with giant lizards in their bedrooms.

Iguanas like to eat green plants, flowers, vegetables, and fruits.

Non-native species of animals have been living in Florida since the 1800s. During the last 30 to 40 years, however, many of our exotic species' populations have grown significantly. I blame the pet trade, as well as the pet owners who decide not to keep their pets—then dump them in the wild. These days, the telephone calls from people who want me to help them with an exotic species just about equal calls for help with our native animals.

The sad truth is that I cannot help all of these animals. Trapping should be a last resort anyway, because it does not solve the problem. Soon enough, another animal will take the trapped animal's place. Sometimes trapping separates animals from their families, leaving orphan babies behind. I cannot rescue all the exotic animals—there are just too many. And I cannot release any I do rescue. I must educate people instead.

Perhaps you have noticed some strange animals in your own neighborhood and wondered what they were and what you should do about them. Maybe you are curious about where these unusual creatures come from, what they like to eat, and whether they might be friendly. Or destructive to Florida's fragile ecosystems. Or even dangerous!

My goal with this book is to help you learn about the exotic wildlife in our midst. Perhaps you will begin to appreciate all the amazing animals we have here in our unique state. I am hoping *Iguana Invasion! Exotic Pets Gone Wild in Florida* will appeal to the animal lover in you.

How to Use This Book

You might be asking yourself: How should we treat the exotic wildlife we find in our backyards? When should we call a trapper for help? Is there anything we can do about the increasing numbers of exotic animals living in Florida? Might we learn to enjoy some of these strange and wonderful animals?

You can find the answers to these questions and more in the chapters that follow. Since there are so many non-native species living here, however, this book will not introduce you to all of them. You can use the References and Resources sections on pages 60 and 62 to explore further. If you are unfamiliar with any of the terms used in the text, you can look these words up in the Glossary on page 64.

Note that the sidebars in this book give you an up-close look at exotic species based on my experience as a wildlife trapper and rehabilitator. Some of the material is my opinion as a humane wildlife professional. The rest of the text is based on factual scientific information from a variety of researchers and resources.

Science evolves over time as new research reveals new facts. For this reason, the information in this book includes estimates taken from many different scientific sources. Some of this information (e.g., the number of species in the state, number of eggs per species, body size of animals, kinds of exotics breeding in Florida) may change as the research on exotics in the wild in Florida continues.

Keep in mind that in biology, animals are named using a formal system. They are given scientific names in a single language: Latin. This system allows scientists all over the world to use the same name for each animal species. In this book, each species is identified by its official English common name, which is capitalized. Also, the animal's scientific or Latin name has been provided for you, and that name is in italics. When referred to in a general way (such as "iguana"), the animal name is neither capitalized nor italicized.

Colorful iguanas add an exotic beauty to the Florida landscape.

Chapter I

Iguana Invasion!

Common Green Iguana

Mexican Spinytail Iguana

Black Spinytail Iguana

There are hundreds of species in the iguana family, and they live in various parts of the world today. Only three species are living and breeding in the wild here in the state of Florida:

■ Common Green Iguana
■ Mexican Spinytail Iguana
■ Black Spinytail Iguana

These three kinds of iguanas are large lizards more than two feet in length. They look like miniature dinosaurs. They were originally pets imported from South America and Central America. All three species are found in the southernmost counties, especially along the coastlines. Some live on islands close to the mainland.

Lizards are reptiles. This means iguanas:

■ have backbones, so they are classified as vertebrates;
■ have scales, which they shed as they grow;
■ lay eggs;
■ are cold-blooded, so they cannot make body heat from the food they eat.

When the temperature drops into the forties, which happens on occasion in Florida, iguanas become sluggish. You can see them falling out of trees! Sometimes they will lie in your driveway or on the street and won't run away even if you come close enough to touch them. Iguanas' bodies cannot create energy when they get this cold. Once the sun warms them, the lizards will recover. If it stays cold for too long, however, these iguanas will die. Forty-degree days are rare in south Florida. That is why it is one of the few areas in the U.S. where they can usually survive in the wild.

There are many predators that will eat iguana babies. Herons, owls, and other birds will eat them. So will raccoons, opossums, rats, and snakes. Your dog or cat might chase down and kill a little iguana just for fun. Once the iguana is fully grown, however, there are no predators in Florida to bother them.

Common Green Iguana *(Iguana iguana)*
You might think the Common Green Iguana, also known as simply the Green Iguana, is always, well, green. The new babies, or "hatch-

Iguanas on the Loose

In 1990, I rescued my first iguana. When a hysterical retiree called me to report a three-foot lizard running around the grounds of her condominium, I could hardly believe it. I thought she must be imagining things. I arrived to see what looked like a prehistoric animal basking on the sun-splashed cement of her patio. When I approached with my net, the bright green lizard rose up on its long legs and loped off like some extinct creature from the Jurassic Park movies!

At the time, I assumed this Common Green Iguana was someone's escaped pet. But then I received a second call, this time from a family in another town. They had an iguana living in one of their palm trees. I began to get call after call, day after day, from people asking for help with Common Green Iguanas all across the county in which I live and work.

Pet stores around the state, it turned out, were doing a booming business selling cute little baby green iguanas. Kids were keeping the seven- or eight-inch babies in aquariums in their bedrooms under special ultraviolet lamps. How fun to watch them grow! And grow, and grow. Uh-oh!

What hundreds of new iguana owners did not realize was that adult Green Iguanas can be as big as six feet in length. And as soon as they reach adolescence, the growing males become aggressive. They don't want to live in a kid's bedroom anymore, and most kids don't want them there. That's why the pet iguana fad of the 1980s turned into an iguana release craze. Parents and their kids dropped off half-grown iguanas in local parks, canals, and neighborhood lakes.

By the 1990s, we had lots of iguanas roaming around. And by 2000, we had an iguana invasion in south Florida!

At first, I was able to respond to the increasing volume of iguana calls. I would trap iguanas and bring them to a local wildlife center that could place them with people who actually liked to keep four- to six-foot lizards as pets. Of course, this was only when I actually succeeded in capturing them, which is difficult because iguanas are super-fast runners and excellent swimmers.

After ten years of chasing iguanas, however, the job became impossible. Now there are thousands, possibly tens of thousands of Green Iguanas living in the wild in south Florida. Every time I trap some of them, more iguanas just take their place. Every year, there are more iguanas living in south Florida.

Green Iguanas turn bright orange during breeding season.

lings," and the growing juveniles are bright green. But the adult iguanas can be brown too, or gray, or even black. When they are breeding, the males turn orange. Adults have black bands on their sides. Their tails are long and also have black bands.

Green Iguanas have a raised ridge called a dorsal crest that runs down the center of the head and back. This crest is bigger on male iguanas. From the neck hangs a funny-looking flap called a dewlap. Green Iguanas wag the dewlap when mating or defending their territory, and it flops around. They also have one large rounded scale on each jowl, which makes them look like a Frankenstein monster!

The Common Green Iguana makes its home in thick trees, usually near water. These iguanas will sleep in tree branches that hang over a lake, pond, canal, or river. You can spot them sunning themselves in palm trees and tall pines. If you chase one, it will run right up a tree trunk to escape. Iguanas will dive into water and swim under the surface for minutes at a time.

Green Iguanas are herbivores. This means they eat only vegetation, like plants, weeds, flowers, fruits, and vegetables. They like to eat brightly colored flowers from plants such as impatiens, bougainvillea, hibiscus, and orchids. All of these are commonly found in Florida yards.

In order to nest, Green Iguanas dig a hole in the ground in which they lay as many as 70 eggs. Lots of animals like to eat these eggs, including crows, raccoons, opossums, and snakes. The baby iguanas that do hatch are around seven inches long. Females that survive to adulthood will grow to four feet in length. Males may reach six or seven feet.

The iguana has a dorsal crest, dewlap, and jowl.

The Common Green Iguana population in Florida is expanding, and their territory is spreading. As the state's winters become milder, iguanas are moving farther north into central Florida. Biologists believe that global warming is contributing to the increase in the areas of Florida that appeal to these lizards.

Baby iguanas may not survive into adulthood.

Both males and females are territorial, so they defend the trees they live in and the surrounding area. This may be your entire backyard! If you get rid of an iguana in your yard, another will soon arrive to replace it and claim the territory as its own. Sometimes iguanas squabble over territory. In a face-off, they perform what looks like head push-ups. They bob their heads at one another, nodding as if to say, "Get lost, man, un-huh, un-huh." They will fight too, so you might even see a brief battle.

Most of the time, Green Iguanas like to bask in the sun on sidewalks and driveways, on docks and pool decks, and in yards and other open spaces. They like to play practical jokes too. They will pee from their hiding places in trees just as you walk beneath them! People in south Florida get pooped on by these pranksters. Boy, can the Green Iguana go! Be careful when you walk underneath any dense tree canopy.

Reptiles

More than 8,000 species of reptile exist in the world today. Florida is home to more species of reptile than any other state in the U.S. Yet Florida has more exotic reptile species than native species.

No matter whether they are native or non-native, reptiles fit into four general categories:

- lizards and snakes (including iguanas)
- turtles (including tortoises and terrapins)
- crocodiles, alligators, and caimans
- tuataras (which are rare lizard-like reptiles found only in New Zealand)

Reptiles tend to be carnivores and will eat insects, bird eggs, and a variety of animals. They can go weeks without eating, and then devour an animal bigger than themselves! Reptiles are cold-blooded vertebrates. They have hard plates or scales as body coverings, and they must rely on the sun to stay warm.

Every year, thousands of wild reptiles are sold as pets in the U.S. Many of these pets die due to lack of proper care or because it is too hard for them to adjust to captivity. In the state of Florida, escapees and released reptiles may thrive in the habitat they find themselves in. Often they will breed.

Mexican Spinytail Iguana
(Ctenosaura pectinata)

You might guess that the Mexican Spinytail Iguana is from Mexico and has a spiny tail. In fact, both of these descriptions are true. This iguana is found in the western and southern parts of Mexico. The only reason Mexican Spinytails are running wild here in Florida is because pet owners let them loose. And they bred. And their offspring bred. Well, you know the story—now a lot of them make their home in the state.

The male Mexican Spinytail is mostly black with white and yellow blotches. Breeding causes the males to turn an orange color. Females have a greenish tint, while babies are bright green with black markings. The adults have a dark head, and their tails are spiked with spines. These spines are actually scales.

The Mexican Spinytail looks a lot like the Black Spinytail Iguana. Wildlife specialists can tell them apart by the markings on their tails, but the two species are often confused.

Mexican Spinytails are smaller than the Green Iguana. Female Mexican Spinytails are usually three feet long, while the males may be up to four feet in length. Hatchlings average seven inches.

Wary and alert, these iguanas are burrow dwellers. The female will lay up to 30 eggs in a burrow she digs in the ground. Both males and females will dig a hole under a sidewalk, cement seawall, or rock pile. There they can hide at night and dart quickly if you approach. Mexican Spinytails are not as fond of the water as the Green Iguana, but will swim away if necessary to escape from you. As babies these iguanas have many predators—the same birds, raccoons, and other animals that will eat the Green Iguana. However, the adult Mexican

The Mexican Spinytail Iguana lives in the Miami area.

Spinytail has no predators.

It is best not to bother the Mexican Spinytail Iguana. They are unfriendly and do not make good pets. This may explain why their owners have released them into the wild.

Most of the Mexican Spinytails in Florida are living in the Miami area and have been since 1972. They have also been reported in Everglades National Park, a popular pet dumping ground.

Black Spinytail Iguana
(Ctenosaura similis)

What do you think: Is the Black Spinytail Iguana black? Well, yes, it is... And no, it's not. *Some* adults are jet black. But the adults can also be brown in color, or tan. Or even yellowish or bluish-gray. When breeding, they may look orange. Their heads are usually brown. Babies are bright green. They darken with age but keep their greenish tint until adulthood.

And yes, there are spiny scales on the tails of the Black Spinytail Iguana. The pattern of these scales helps wildlife experts determine the species. The Black Spinytail is smaller than the Mexican Spinytail, typically growing to two or three feet in length. Out in the wild, however, it can be difficult to tell the two species of spinytail iguanas apart. The Black Spinytail is native to southern Mexico and Central America. This type of iguana lives in the wild here in Florida because some pet owners decided not to be responsible for them anymore. Once the iguanas were released, they went on to live and breed in the wild.

The Black Spinytail poses a big threat to Florida's native species and its ecosystem. Black Spinytail Iguanas live in burrows under the concrete foundations of homes and seawalls, in sand dunes, and on construction sites.

The Black Spinytail Iguana can be a problem on islands where it is not native.

Problems on Gasparilla Island

A tourist destination off the southwest coast of Florida, Gasparilla is a lovely little barrier island in the Gulf of Mexico. The island is seven miles long and has a small population of full-time residents.

Gasparilla is also home to thousands of Black Spinytail Iguanas!

According to the locals, sometime during the 1970s a resident brought back from Mexico three iguanas for his children. When these Black Spinytails were no longer wanted, he released them onto public land and forgot all about them. By the 1990s, there were a few thousand offspring of the three iguanas living on Gasparilla. Most residents regarded them as harmless.

Over the next ten years, though, the population of Black Spintyail Iguanas exploded to more than 12,000! Islanders complained that the iguanas were ruining their landscaping, sparking power outages, digging up seawalls, and ripping down screening. People reported that iguanas were nesting in their attics, even appearing in their toilets!

Environmentalists are concerned that the Black Spinytail Iguanas are reducing the sea turtle populations. They are worried because these iguanas compete with the native snakes and birds for food, and with Gopher Tortoises for nesting sites. The iguanas may be weakening the sand dunes that help to protect the island during hurricanes.

The Chamber of Commerce on Gasparilla Island does not like the impact that the presence of so many large lizards has had on tourists. Everybody complains about the iguana droppings: Too much poop!

In 2006, the islanders hired a wildlife biologist to study the problem and a wildlife trapper to reduce the iguana population. The biologist has recommended controlling the iguanas' winter food source, a non-native plant called the Brazilian pepper tree. These bushes bloom in the winter, and they offer a bright red fruit the iguanas can eat when other plants are not in bloom. Limiting the number of those bushes could help keep the iguana population in check too. The biologist has also advised closing off the iguanas' nesting burrows to prevent eggs from hatching. He has suggested attacking the iguanas in the winter when it is cold and they slow down. The wildlife trapper claims he has captured and euthanized thousands of iguanas. But he admits that many thousands still live freely on the island.

The Black Spinytail Iguana has been sighted on neighboring islands. Perhaps the iguanas swim there, or hitchhike over on boats. Who can blame them for trying to escape? Some have been seen on the Florida mainland. People have reported finding iguanas that have crawled up under car hoods to catch a ride off the island!

The resident who released his children's pets so many years ago did not realize this would happen. He had no idea a few stray pets could evolve into such a massive mess. All over the state of Florida, *pet owners are unaware of the potential problems caused by letting pets go wild*.

The female will lay one to two dozen eggs in the burrows she digs in the ground. These iguanas like to sun themselves on rock piles, logs, or on top of sand dunes. They are shy and will dart into their burrows if you approach. Or they will swim away, though they are not as fond of the water as the Green Iguana. They may hiss at you if you corner them, and will scratch if trapped.

Babies and juveniles are eaten by snakes, birds, and raccoons. The adult Black Spinytail Iguana, however, has no predators. Although they mostly forage for plants and flowers, fruits and greens, these iguanas are carnivores, or meat eaters. They will eat small vertebrates like other lizards, sea turtle eggs and hatchlings, bird eggs, and nestlings. They will use other species' burrows, forcing native animals like Gopher Tortoises to seek shelter elsewhere. For these reasons, the Black Spinytail Iguana is regarded as an undesirable "invasive" species.

You might find this iguana hunting through your garbage for scraps. Or it may dig burrows under your house or seawall. That is bad because those burrows might weaken the structure of the house or wall. For these reasons, some Florida communities currently regard the Black Spinytail Iguana as a serious invasive pest.

What We Can Do

The situation on Gasparilla Island is unique. However, south Florida residents are complaining more about the iguanas as their numbers increase. Some cities now consider the Green Iguana a nuisance species and are looking for ways to reduce the population. All three species of iguana living and breeding in our state scare people. Iguanas can look pretty frightening if you don't know what these lizards are or what should be done when you see a big reptile sitting in your yard.

There is no reason to be scared of iguanas. They do not attack humans, so if you don't bother them, they won't bother you. It is best not to call in a trapper every time you see an iguana. If caught, the iguana will have to be killed. And soon enough, another iguana will replace it and claim the territory as his or her own.

But if you decide you want to keep the iguanas out of your home and yard, you can make certain changes that seem to help. Here are some steps your family can take in order to "iguana proof" your home:

- Remove any colorful flowering plants from your yard.
- Remove fruit trees from your yard (except citrus, which they won't eat).
- If you leave fruit trees in your yard, pick up ripe fruit that has fallen to the ground.
- Do not plant a vegetable garden in your yard, or if you do, screen it in.
- Cut back tree canopy and keep trees thinned.
- Trim trees away from your house and roof.
- Trim trees away from your dock and pool.
- Tie plastic bottles on your boat line so iguanas cannot climb up to your boat.
- Install sheet metal on dock pilings so iguanas cannot climb up.
- Use a child-proof fence around your swimming pool deck to keep iguanas out.
- Spray garlic oil around your yard (they don't like the scent).

- Expose hiding spots by keeping your yard free of brush and debris.
- Let your dog roam the yard to scare off wildlife.

You can spray any visiting iguanas with a garden hose. They don't like this and may decide to find a more welcoming property to call their own.

If all this effort seems like a lot of work, you might decide to befriend the iguanas in your neighborhood instead. If you already have flowers, vegetables, or fruit growing in your yard, they may come over for the "free buffet." When the iguanas appear, don't chase them, corner them, or yell at them. If you want to approach, always move slowly. Once they know you are friendly, the iguanas may let you get close enough to see their unique natures.

Iguanas are fascinating animals. If you treat them with respect, the iguanas living in your neighborhood may find you interesting too.

Iguanas like to relax in the sun.

Chapter 2
Other Lizards on the Loose

Brown Anole

In the state of Florida there are more than 30 exotic lizard species currently living in the wild. A large number of these are tiny geckos and anoles (pronounced an-o-lees). Most of the species are expanding their populations. And the majority of them can be found in the urban areas of south Florida, where it is warm most of the year.

All of these exotic lizard species were originally brought to Florida for sale as pets, or they arrived on boats from other countries, hidden in cargo. These non-native lizards were released into the wild either by accident or on purpose, an illegal act in Florida and many other states. Readily adapting to our pleasant environment, the exotic lizards have settled in to stay—and to breed.

Unlike the three species of iguana, however, the other exotic lizards living and breeding in Florida do not get much attention. Most of these lizards are small, usually measured in inches. When you walk across the sidewalk you can see the small anoles scurry out of the way to hide in bushes or crevices in the cement. Little geckos can be found inside your

house, running straight up the walls or hiding behind pictures or cabinets. Floridians are used to having the little lizards around us, so we often ignore them.

However, these exotic lizards are probably competing with our native species for food and territory. Scientists warn that the large populations of non-native lizards are impacting our native lizards, significantly reducing their numbers. For example, the Green Anole *(Anolis carolinensis)*, a once abundant Florida native, has become less common. Meanwhile, its main competitor, the exotic Brown Anole *(Anolis sagrei)*, can be found everywhere in the state in great numbers.

Since they are so widespread, it would be impossible to remove all of the non-native lizards that are living and breeding on their own in Florida. Like our exotic iguanas, these smaller lizards have become a part of Florida's new fauna. They are here to stay.

Fortunately, the smaller exotic lizards are typically harmless—and interesting. You might want to seek out some of the unusual lizard species roaming around your neighborhood.

Bedroom Surprise

Opossums, or "possums" as we call the furry gray mammals here in Florida, live all over the state. I get many calls from people who regard these harmless native animals as pests. This is because the possum will eat almost anything, including pet food left outside and table scraps out of easily opened garbage cans. Usually I tell callers how to keep possums out of their yards in the future. If an animal is trapped inside the home, however, I will come out to remove it.

One day I went on what I thought would be a routine trip to trap an opossum. When I arrived at the elderly woman's house on the edge of the Everglades, her live-in nurse greeted me in the driveway. She seemed terrified. I spoke calmly to her, explaining how I would simply throw a beach towel over the possum. This would quiet the animal so I could pick it up and place it in a transport cage. Then I could return the frightened animal to the woods where it belonged.

The nurse relaxed a little and told me she had only *heard* the animal rustling around in her closet. She hadn't actually *seen* it. Her employer had called in a neighbor, who had peeked into the nurse's bedroom. The neighbor spotted what he said was a possum. The two women then took his advice and called me.

No problem.

The women waited outside while I grabbed a towel from my van and entered the house through the garage. Both the garage door and the door into the house from the garage were wide open. This was most likely the route the animal had taken to get inside the house. Animals will venture into an open garage looking for food, then stumble into the house through another open door.

The nurse's bedroom door was closed, so I opened it slowly and quietly. Nothing. No rustle, no scurry, no musky wild animal scent. I walked into the room, heading toward the closet, the towel ready in my arms.

Suddenly I heard behind me the scratch of claws on tile. I turned to face an angry tegu. This South American lizard is the size of a dog. The tegu was jet black with white spots. It poked its split tongue at me like a menacing snake in attack mode.

Just another day in the life of a wildlife trapper in Florida, where exotic pets run wild and free.

The tegu I captured was black and white like this one.

A common sight on streets and sidewalks, the Northern Curlytail Lizard (*Leiocephalus carinatus armouri*) can be identified by its spiral tail.

If you pay close attention, you will see that not all of the little lizards scurrying across the sidewalks of your town are the same.

Certain large species of non-native lizards in Florida should be avoided for safety reasons.

Tokay Gecko (*Gekko gecko*)

The Tokay Gecko is a brightly colored lizard from Southeast Asia. These feisty lizards were originally imported and sold as pets. They have adapted to living in the wild in Hawaii, Texas, Florida, and a few other places. They live in trees and dine on other lizards, frogs, and various insects.

You will know a Tokay Gecko if you see or hear one. They are an unmistakable blue-gray color with red-orange spots. These strange lizards are also nocturnal. The males make a loud call at night that sounds like "tokay" or "uh-oh." Adults can be about 12 inches in length. As pets, these lizards have been known to bite the hand that feeds them—and not let go until they are dunked in water!

Florida's Geckos

Geckos are small- to average-size lizards without eyelids. There are around 2,000 different species of geckos living in warm climates around the world. Many of these species have specialized toe pads. These allow the lizards to walk on walls and ceilings! Geckos can be found hunting for insects to eat. They will gather near the lights inside or outside our homes and under street lamps. Their tails can break off and grow back, and their skin is thin and easily shed. These two special characteristics allow geckos to slip away from predators, leaving a tail or some skin behind.

Florida is home to only one native species of gecko. The Florida Reef Gecko (*Sphaerodactylus notatus notatus*) is a tiny, very shy lizard, so you won't often see one. But geckos are a common sight in Florida because there are more than ten species of exotics living and breeding in the state. Whenever you see these lizards clinging to the walls of your house or hanging off your front door at night, you can be pretty sure they are members of an exotic species.

The various species of exotic geckos living and breeding in the wild in Florida come from the West Indies, Central and South America, South Africa, Southeast Asia, and elsewhere. Some are released and escaped pets. Others arrived hidden on cargo ships. These geckos compete with one another for food and territory.

If you want to look for geckos, the best time to observe them is at night. Quietly approach an outdoor light such as a front porch lamp or a street lamp with insects buzzing around in the glare. You might be able to see exotic geckos hanging on the wall, door, or post, maybe even snapping up prey.

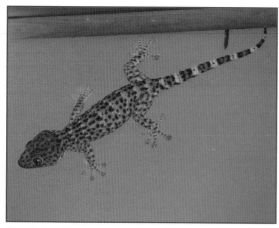

The Tokay Gecko is imported from Southeast Asia.

You can understand why some pet owners decide they no longer wish to own these lizards once they reach adult size. If you see a Tokay Gecko in the wild, do not go up to it. If cornered, this lizard may bite.

Knight Anole *(Anolis equestris)*

The Knight Anole is native to Cuba. This anole looks like a smaller version of the Common Green Iguana. The Knight Anole, however, has a triangular head, and its tail is extra long. The bright green body of this lizard is marked by yellow slashes. Its dewlap, the flap on its neck, is pale pink. Adults are typically 12 to 20 inches long. In Miami, Spanish-speaking residents call the Knight Anole an "iguanito," which means "little iguana."

When this lizard is cold or stressed, it turns dark brown. So some people may mistakenly call the Knight Anole a chameleon. It is not.

Knight Anoles live high up in the tops of trees. You may not notice them because they like to stay hidden in the leafy tree canopy. Sometimes you can spot a Knight Anole on a tree trunk. It will cling to the trunk, its head facing the ground, while basking in the sun.

Or you might see this lizard sneaking across phone lines, traveling from tree top to tree top.

The Knight Anole is a carnivore. They eat mostly large insects and fruit, but they will also prey on frogs, anoles, geckos, small birds, bird eggs, and hatchlings. They have sharp teeth and can injure birds as large as doves.

When cornered, these large anoles will stand their ground. If frightened, they will bite their attackers. It is best to watch these lizards from a distance.

In south Florida, Knight Anoles living in the wild are released and abandoned pets, or

The Knight Anole will sun itself on the trunks of trees.

their offspring. In the 1950s, a student at the University of Miami uncaged his pet Knight Anoles. They settled in the city, where they gradually formed a small population. By the early 1990s, wild Knight Anoles had been reported as far south as Key West. Since then, the Knight Anole has become more abundant throughout the southern areas of our state.

The Knight Anole does not make a good pet. They seem so cute as babies, but these anoles become unruly and aggressive as they get older. Once you are stuck with an undesirable pet, it is tempting to let it loose in a nearby park. Then you become part of the problem created by exotics in Florida.

Nile Monitor *(Varanus niloticus)*

There are more than 30 species of monitor lizards living around the world, including the famous 10-foot-long Komodo Dragon of Indonesia. The Nile Monitor is from Africa. In fact, it is the largest lizard living on the African continent. Adults may grow to more than seven feet.

Since the early 1990s, Nile Monitors have been sighted living in the wild in south Florida. That would make them the largest lizards living in the wild in the U.S. These giant lizards are escaped or abandoned pets and their descendants.

The Nile Monitor is gray or brown with darker bands and several gold-colored bands. Before they reach adulthood, Nile Monitors are black and white. These lizards have a remarkable tongue that is split at the tip. Like snakes, the Monitor lizard will warn off predators by flicking its forked tongue and hissing.

The Nile Monitor likes to live near water. In Florida, these exotics may be found in marshes and swamps and on the banks of rivers, lakes, or canals. They will hide in burrows they have dug in the ground or stolen from other burrowing animals. The female lays as many as 60 eggs in these burrows.

A large and aggressive lizard, the Nile Monitor is ill-suited to life as a pet.

Problems in Cape Coral

A breeding population of Nile Monitors has become a problem for the residents of Cape Coral, in southwest Florida. Hundreds of these lizards are traveling around this lovely city by way of the many man-made canals. It is likely the Nile Monitors were once pets that outgrew their welcome and were let go.

The giant lizards are strong swimmers, fast runners, and good climbers. People in Cape Coral complain that Nile Monitors are lying on their roofs, pool decks, and sea walls. Scientists from the University of Florida have been conducting research on possible ways to eliminate the lizard problem.

Nile Monitors have been reported on some of Cape Coral's neighboring islands. The lizards use the canals to travel for many miles. They have been seen in other areas of mainland south Florida as well. Researchers are worried that the Nile Monitor may make its way throughout Florida.

Monitor lizards do not make good pets. They need room-size cages and lots of food. They are wild animals that get nervous in captivity, and they will bite. Their teeth are sharp. Unwanted pet Nile Monitor lizards should never be let loose.

Just ask the people living in Cape Coral.

Monitors are carnivores. The Nile Monitor eats crabs, mussels, fish, frogs, lizards, turtles, snakes, birds, eggs, and small mammals. They will eat table scraps and garbage. In Africa, they are known to eat house cats!

Because of its size and diet, the Nile Monitor is considered an invasive species in Florida. These lizards can impact the native species we are trying to protect, including Gopher Tortoises, nesting sea turtles, and birds like Burrowing Owls. The Nile Monitor may also dig up the eggs of our native alligators and crocodiles.

If you see a Nile Monitor on the loose in your neighborhood, it is a good idea to report it to a local wildlife center. You should call a humane trapper if this large lizard is in your yard. Keep your cats and dogs inside until the Monitor has been captured. You may also want to report your sighting to the Florida Fish and Wildlife Conservation Commission on their wildlife hotline (see Resources on page 62). *Never approach a wild Nile Monitor on your own.*

Tegus

Various species of these large and scary looking lizards are brought from South America to the U.S. to be sold as pets. Popular with the pet trade are the Red Tegu *(Tupinambis rufescens)*, the Argentine Black and White Tegu *(Tupinambis merianae)*, and the Common Tegu *(Tupinambis teguixin)*. Hatchlings are six to eight inches long. Adults may be more than four feet in length. The cute little babies grow quickly. They develop sharp teeth and claws, as well as a long forked tongue.

Escaped and abandoned tegus have adapted to living on their own in south Florida, although there is no evidence they are breeding. This does not mean that they are not breeding in the wild in Florida. It only means that wildlife biologists have not yet formally reported on the tegus living in the wild.

The tegu is a tropical animal and will not survive cold winters. It is rare to see a tegu on the loose in suburban areas. However, Common Tegus have been reported living in parks in south Florida, including Everglades National Park.

Pet tegus eat mostly mice, insects, and fruit. Out in the wild in Florida, they probably feed on small animals as well. This might include baby birds, turtles, and other lizards and their eggs.

The tegu is an agile climber and swimmer. These lizards are fast on their feet and have a powerful bite. They are excitable, and tend to fear humans. If you see a tegu on the loose, call a licensed humane wildlife trapper. Don't try to capture these lizards on your own.

A baby tegu is often advertised as a "friendly" lizard, but it can bite.

Tegus have sharp teeth and forked tongues, and they grow to more than four feet in length.

Pet Trade

On a recent visit to a local pet store, I met a young family who lived in the area. They had come to the store with the hope of returning their unwanted reptile. "When we bought it here six months ago, it was tiny and cute," the mother explained. "Now we're all afraid of it."

When one of the store employees released the three-foot Red Tegu from its carrier, both children ran down the aisles to hide. "I'm scared whenever Big Red is out of her cage," the 10-year-old girl said. Then she ducked behind me as the store employee, who was wearing special gloves, began to stroke the lizard softly. The tegu flicked its long tongue.

"We had a Nile Monitor lizard," the mother said, "but it escaped. And we never found it."

It is unfair to keep large lizards in small cages or, worse, bathrooms.

This pet Red Tegu was no longer wanted once it grew to adult size.

Over the years, I have rescued large lizards from suburban bathrooms, where the frightened owners have trapped their fast-growing pets. **This is not fair to the animals.** If you think you want to own an exotic reptile as a pet, it is important to do some research first. Find out how big the animal gets, what kind of habits it will have as an adult, and if it might be dangerous to humans. Remember that most wild animals do not enjoy living in cages or aquariums. Or bathrooms! And letting them loose is never an option.

Chapter 3

Boas, Pythons, and More Sneaky Surprises

Common Boa

Green Anaconda

African Ball Python

Snakes are long, narrow vertebrates without legs. All snakes are reptiles. Some legless lizards resemble snakes, but snakes are supple and muscular while lizards have rigid bodies. Most snakes can relax their jaws to swallow prey larger than their heads. Lizards cannot do this.

If a snake is more than ten feet in length, it is usually a boa or a python. In Florida, no native snakes are this large. Only escaped and abandoned pets are this enormous.

Some scientists consider boas and pythons to be part of a single classification. Other biologists separate the two. There are 43 species in the boa family, including the Common Boa of Central and South America and the Green Anaconda of Trinidad and northern South America. Pythons come from Asia, Africa, Australia, and the islands nearby. The breeding habits of boas and pythons are different. Unlike most reptiles, female boas do not lay eggs. Instead, they give birth to live young.

Common Boa (*Boa constrictor*)

The Common Boa is a yellow, gray, or light brown snake with dark brown patterning. Some have reddish markings on the tail. These snakes are carnivorous, feeding on small to medium-sized birds and mammals. Common Boas hunt for prey on the ground and in trees. They are active at twilight and during the night.

The Common Boa is a non-venomous snake. It is an easygoing, adaptable animal that will breed readily in captivity. This is why these boas are popular pets. Once a year, the female will give birth to as many as 50 live babies. They can be friendly when raised by humans. For that reason, they are advertised by the pet trade for use in films, television, and entertainment parks. In the wild, baby snakes have many predators and not all will survive. Once they are fully grown, Common Boas may reach a length of 13 feet! In the wild in Florida, these large snakes have no predators.

When people living in Florida tire of their pet reptiles, they may choose to dump them in areas they imagine resemble the jungle. This is why Everglades National Park is home to lots of former pets. So are some of the parks around the city of Miami and elsewhere in south Florida. The warm winters allow tropical snakes like the Common Boa to survive there.

Very large snakes are not frequent eaters because their metabolism, or body processing rate, is slow. For these reptiles to digest food takes a long time, so they may go for weeks between feedings. When they do eat, however, these big snakes will consume native wildlife. This could include threatened and endangered species. Large snakes will also compete with Florida's native snakes for food and territory.

Super-Size It!

Snakes were never my favorite animal. Once I became a humane trapper and wildlife rehabilitator, however, getting close to these reptiles was part of my job. Over the years, I have learned to appreciate snakes, their beauty and strength. I am also respectful of the serious dangers posed by some of the exotic species currently on the loose in our state.

In fact, the biggest snake I ever attempted to capture is still on the loose. Last time I saw it, this enormous exotic snake was only a few miles from my house.

The city police contacted me late one autumn afternoon. They were calling from a park that was being built next to a big canal. The park surveyors had spotted a very large snake hiding in piles of debris.

I hurried over in my van. Two burly policemen and three city employees were standing near a dry area of the canal. All five stared at me as I approached. There was fear on their faces.

The massive snake had an olive brown coloring with black markings, so it blended in perfectly with the branches and leaves around it. It looked to be more than 15 feet long. The body was as wide as a basketball.

I've seen some big snakes in my life, including captive exotic species in zoos and at wildlife centers. This snake was the biggest I've ever seen. This snake was super-sized!

For several hours I attempted to net the snake's head with my monkey net. I stumbled over tree roots and broken branches. The huge animal just slithered in and out of the thick underbrush smoothly and gracefully. The snake was in its element. I was not.

Finally, one of the policemen attempted to assist me by gripping the body of the huge reptile with his bare hands. His partner moved in to help. I started to warn the two men that this was a very dangerous thing to do since I had not been able to net the head yet. And that's when it happened.

The snake musked.

Musk is an oily, smelly discharge some snakes can release from under the tail when they are trying to defend themselves. If you have never smelled snake musk, just imagine the combined odors of old sneakers, week-old garbage, and rotting roadkill. Musk from a big snake smells worse than that. Much worse.

Both of the policemen were splashed with the orange-brown slime. We were all coughing and gagging. The snake took advantage of our distraction and slipped away into the night. As I watched it disappear into the underbrush, I felt a renewed sense of respect for snakes.

When constrictor snakes kill their prey, they squeeze the animal until it is crushed to death. Common Boas also strike with their heads, and their teeth can make serious wounds. These snakes can eat a small dog or cat. They have been found hiding under car hoods, where they wrap around the engine. One unlucky Floridian discovered a Common Boa in his engine after the snake had wrapped around the accelerator and caused his car to speed wildly!

If you see what you think is a Common Boa in your neighborhood, do not approach the snake. It is best to go inside and call a licensed humane wildlife trapper. Once the snake is netted, the trapper will bring it to a wildlife center that seeks adoptive homes for exotic snakes.

Owning a baby snake may seem fun and easy. You just keep the snake in an aquarium in your bedroom and feed it a dead mouse once in a while to freak out your friends, right? But what happens when the little snake gets big? What about when it is bigger than you and your friends are, and it needs to eat bunny rabbits for dinner? And what happens to your huge snake when you grow up and leave home for work or college?

Adopting an animal is a serious responsibility. It is important to think about your desire for a "fun" pet and whether it's worth the years of responsibilities owning a large exotic snake will require.

Green Anaconda (Eunectes murinus)

All of the really giant snakes in the world are either boas or pythons. Anacondas are a kind of boa. But they are much larger than the Common Boa.

Anacondas are also called "water boas" and are non-poisonous constrictors. They bite their prey to hold it in place while squeezing the animal to suffocate it. Anacondas are the widest and heaviest snakes in the world.

Of the four species of anacondas, two are rare and two are more common. The Green Anaconda is one of the common species. In fact, it is also called the Common Anaconda. These snakes are the largest of the anacondas, and they may grow to 35 feet in length! The average Green Anaconda is 20 feet long, weighs more than 300 pounds, and is more than 12 inches in diameter.

The Green Anaconda has been found living in the wild in Florida. Whenever a Green Anaconda is on the loose in our state, it is a released or escaped pet. These massive snakes have been seen in Everglades National Park and nearby in Big Cypress Swamp, a U.S. national preserve. It is unknown whether these snakes are breeding.

The Green Anaconda is shy and will flee humans whenever possible.

Green Anacondas like to live near the water, where they will lie in wait for prey. They are dark olive green in color, with black spots and rings. Their coloring provides excellent camouflage for hiding on the banks of rivers or canals and in branches of trees above the water. Sometimes they sink down into water up to their eyes while waiting for prey to come for a drink.

The Green Anaconda will eat herons, turtles, pigs, deer, and other large animals. Their jaws and skin are flexible enough to allow them to eat animals as large as full-grown jaguars. A big meal may take months to digest. These snakes can go for a year between meals!

When disturbed, an anaconda will swim away or sink to the bottom of a body of water and wait for long periods. As a second line of defense, the Green Anaconda may musk. This is when they give off an orange-brown, terribly smelly substance.

You do not want to meet a Green Anaconda loose in your neighborhood!

Fortunately, these snakes are not popular pets. Even zookeepers find that these snakes are too bad tempered in captivity. It is unlikely that you will see a Green Anaconda in your yard. But if you do see a massive snake, do not go up to it. Keep your dogs and cats inside and call the police. You can dial the emergency number (911) and report what you have seen. The police will come to guard the snake and keep people away from it until a wildlife trapper arrives. A licensed humane wildlife trapper can take the snake to a wildlife center that accepts giant exotic snakes.

Burmese Python
(Python molurus bivittatus)

There are ten different species of python. These species include the Burmese Python, the African Rock Python (Python sebae), and the smaller African Ball Python (Python regius). All of these species are sold by the pet trade, but the Burmese Python is the most popular.

Native to southeast Asia, the Burmese Python can now be seen sunning itself on the roads of south Florida. Since the 1980s, these large exotic snakes have been reported living and breeding in the wild in Miami, the Keys, and Everglades National Park. All of these pythons are escaped or abandoned pets and their offspring.

The Burmese Python is thick and long. It can grow to 25 or 26 feet in length. These snakes are tan, brown, and white in a boxy pattern.

Loose pet African Ball Pythons may be breeding in the wild in Florida. These pythons rarely grow to more than four feet in length, and will roll into a ball when stressed or frightened.

In the wild, the Burmese Python likes to live near water. They are fast snakes, and are excellent swimmers and climbers. These snakes can snatch their prey quite easily. They will prey on reptiles, mammals, and birds. Here in Florida, these pythons eat rabbits, squirrels, raccoons, and wading birds like herons and their hatchlings. Because they are so large, these snakes eat a lot of food and therefore threaten a variety of the wildlife species in our state.

The Burmese Python is a popular pet due to its "gentle giant" reputation.

The Python Problem

The python population in Florida is expanding. From 2002 to 2005, more than 200 pythons were captured here. From 2006 to 2007, over 400 of these exotic snakes were caught in the wild. They are breeding here, and will migrate, or move, many miles over land or in the water.

Everglades National Park is a popular dumping spot for unwanted snakes. Because of the significant increase in pythons on the loose there, a Python Hotline has been established. It allows visitors to the park to report sightings. Trappers are called in to capture the snakes, a difficult job. All trapped pythons are euthanized.

Several fights between Florida alligators and exotic pythons have been reported. In one instance, a passerby recorded the battle on video, including the swallowing of the python by the gator. Native crocodiles, too, have been seen eating pythons in the wild in Florida. However, large pythons are able to eat alligators and crocodiles. Therefore, we cannot rely on our native reptiles to reduce the growing python population in our state.

The Burmese Python causes problems in the wild in Florida.

In the Florida Keys, scientists are attempting to halt a Burmese Python invasion. They believe the snakes are moving there from the Everglades.

The invading exotics are eating native wildlife, including several rare species that live on these islands. For example, Burmese Pythons are preying on the federally endangered Key Largo Woodrat *(Neotoma floridana smalli)*. The exotic snakes also compete with our native snakes for food and territory. This includes the federally endangered Eastern Indigo Snake *(Drymarchon corais couperi)*. This eight-foot-long, non-venomous species is the largest snake native to the U.S.

A program has been established in the Keys to keep the population of exotic snakes from getting out of control on the islands. The program teaches people what to do when they see a Burmese Python sunning itself on the side of the road. A hotline has been set up for reporting sightings. Workshops have been held to instruct residents who do a lot of driving, including postal workers, meter readers, those who work in road construction, and lawn-care crews. Volunteers are taught to stay at a safe distance and to watch the snake until trappers arrive.

Sadly, any pythons that are trapped this way will be euthanized. This is unfair to the snakes. After all, these exotic animals are not to blame for their release into an environment that allows them to prosper while threatening the native inhabitants.

In 2009, several African Rock Pythons on the loose were trapped in neighborhoods west of Miami. One was a female carrying 37 eggs, another was a juvenile. This could mean a breeding population. Wildlife experts are concerned since these giant snakes are nervous and aggressive.

However, it is often abandoned when it reaches adult size. A huge snake is difficult to handle and expensive to feed. Unfortunately, pet owners in Florida let their exotic snakes loose in our local and state parks. This is, of course, against the law.

If you see a Burmese Python on the loose, be sure to stay back. Call 911 and carefully explain where you saw the snake. The police will guard it until a wildlife trapper arrives.

Even though these snakes are not poisonous, they can bite. Be sure to keep your dog or cat away from these large exotic snakes. Burmese Pythons can swallow an 18-pound pet cat or dog whole! In 2009, an escaped pet Burmese Python killed a 2-year-old child in a small town in central Florida.

Reticulated Python
(Python reticulatus)

The Reticulated Python is the largest of the ten python species. These snakes can grow to lengths of more than 30 feet! They are not as wide and heavy as the Green Anaconda, but they can grow to similar lengths.

The Reticulated Python is native to southeast Asia and the islands near Australia. It is the largest snake in Asia. The netted patterns on the back of this snake are called "reticulations." This means large spots separated by narrow white lines.

These huge snakes feed on birds and mammals. They have heat sensors in their jaws that help them locate prey. Unlike boas, pythons lay eggs. The Reticulated Python may lay as many as 100 eggs. The female coils around them until they hatch. Large birds will prey on the young snakes, but a full-grown python has few predators.

These snakes do not make good pets. They are massive in size and require live animals for their diet. Reticulated Pythons are aggressive and will bite, although they are not poisonous. There have been reports of Reticulated Pythons attacking and killing humans, but none in the state of Florida.

In the wild, Reticulated Pythons may outcompete our native wildlife for food and

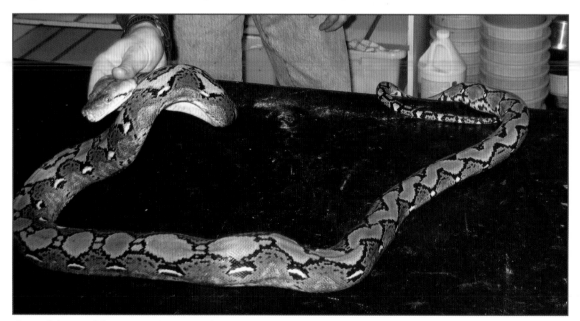

One of the world's giant snakes is the Reticulated Python.

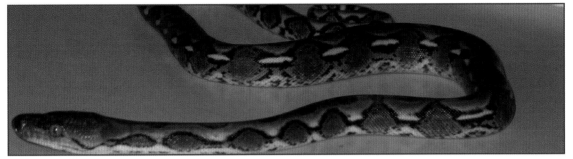

Juvenile Reticulated Pythons are small and pretty.

territory. Because they are so massive, these exotic snakes consume a lot of food. They may be part of the reason for the decline in our native wildlife populations, including the species that are threatened or endangered.

If you ever see an enormous snake like the Reticulated Python, do not go near it. Immediately report your finding to the police. They will guard the snake and call for a Wildlife Trapper to try to capture it.

Of course, capture is not always possible with these monstrous snakes. Escaped or released pets with the size and power of Reticulated Pythons, Burmese Pythons, and anacondas are a danger to all of us. As residents of Florida, where the world's largest snakes are able to survive on their own and reproduce in the wild, we must *avoid buying large exotic snakes as pets.*

Don't get fooled by pet-trade advertisements for "tame" and "friendly" exotic snakes. Those cute little baby snakes will grow into large, expensive, difficult, and possibly dangerous adults.

The African Rock Python is easily mistaken for the Burmese Python. The African Rock Python is less popular as a pet and more hostile toward humans.

Chapter 4

Killer Toads and Other Strange Pests

Greenhouse Frog

You read about exotic snakes and lizards in chapters One, Two, and Three. In addition to those animals, there are two other non-native reptiles on the loose that are having an impact on our state. The Red-Eared Slider Turtle and the Spectacled Caiman are both popular pets. Both of these exotic reptiles pose a threat to the Florida ecosystem when they are released.

Red-Eared Slider Turtle
(*Trachemys scripta elegans*)

Also known as the "pond slider," the Red-Eared Slider Turtle is the most common pet turtle sold in the U.S. These turtles are green in color with black and tan markings. They have a bright red slash mark behind each eye.

The Red-Eared Slider is a non-marine turtle. This means they do not live in sea water. Instead, they make their home in brackish water, which is a mix of sea water and fresh water. They prefer to live near canals or ponds, which are quiet bodies of water with soft bot-

toms and plenty of plants. You can see them in lakes and rivers, too, basking in the sun while lying on rocks or logs. Sometimes several will pile on top of one another in a turtle mound.

Red slash marks on the head help to identify the Red-Eared Slider Turtle.

The Red-Eared Slider Turtle's diet consists mainly of vegetation. But these turtles will eat insects, fish and shellfish, snails, worms, and small lizards. They will eat dog and cat food, too. They have no teeth and must bite with the sharp, bony edges of their mouths.

Like all turtles, the Red-Eared Slider lives in the water and may remain underwater for as long as an hour. These turtles lay their eggs on land. The survival rate of the baby turtles is low. They are often eaten by birds, crabs, and other predators. But the adult Red-Eared Slider Turtle has few predators in Florida.

Native to the Mississippi River, these turtles are the most widespread non-marine turtle in the world. This is because they are such common and commonly abandoned pets. Since they compete with native turtles wherever they are released, the Red-Eared Slider is considered a nuisance species around the globe.

Most of the escaped exotics originally came from turtle farms in the United States, where millions are raised for the international pet trade. However, many countries, including the European Union, do not allow these pet turtles to be imported anymore. This is because of the negative impact on native wildlife.

A highly adaptable turtle, the Red-Eared Slider can live in a variety of environments. As pets, the juveniles like to eat animal-based food. The adults prefer vegetation. Once they are released into the wild, however, these turtles can adjust to most habitats and will eat whatever is available. This is called "generalization." Animals that are generalists can live almost anywhere and eat almost anything. For this reason, generalists usually outcompete animals that can handle only a specific kind of habitat or food. Those animals are called "specialists." The specialist will become extinct while the generalist thrives.

In Florida, the Red-Eared Slider is interbreeding with some of our native species of turtles. Here is the typical story: A kid buys a cute little Red-Eared Slider for a few dollars and keeps it in an aquarium in his or her bedroom. The kid feeds the turtle and gives it a cute name. One day, however, the kid notices that the turtle is getting too big for its home. When the turtle grows to 10 or 12 inches, the kid decides to give the adult turtle its "freedom" by letting it loose in a nearby park. There, the adaptable pet can feed and breed, possibly interbreeding with the native Florida species of non-marine turtles.

It is too late to remove this exotic species from our state. The Red-Eared Slider Turtle has become another member of Florida's new fauna, or animal environment. Still, you might want to avoid purchasing a Red-Eared Slider as a pet.

And if you do have one as a pet, **never release it into the wild**.

Also, be aware that turtles from turtle farms may have salmonella, which is a disease-causing bacteria. It is best not to handle these turtles with your bare hands. In fact, children's doctors do not recommend adopting pet turtles for households with young children. The elderly and people with serious illnesses probably should not buy these turtles either for health reasons.

Spectacled Caiman
(Caiman crocodilus)

Alligators, crocodiles, and the smaller alligators known as caimans are all reptiles of considerable size. They are carnivores and can eat large prey. This includes full-grown turtles and snakes, big fish, and small mammals. Since they are cold-blooded, caimans spend a lot of time basking in the sun and digesting huge meals.

The American Alligator *(Alligator mississippiensis)* and the American Crocodile *(Crocodylus acutus)* are native to Florida. Both range from 8 to 12 feet in length. The alligator has a rounded snout, while the crocodile has a more pointed nose.

The Spectacled Caiman is usually no more than 6 feet long. Adults are olive green with darker bands. Unlike the larger alligator and crocodile, the caiman has a U-shaped bony bump between the eyes. This species is not native to Florida. It comes from Central America and northern South America. The Spectacled Caimans seen in the Florida wild are released pets and their offspring.

Alligators are abundant in Florida, especially in parks with canals, rivers, swamps, and other bodies of fresh or brackish water. Crocodiles are less common in Florida. Still, they are occasionally seen in Everglades National Park, the Keys, and in large parks around the southern tip of the state. The American Crocodile is an endangered species and is federally protected.

The non-native Spectacled Caiman is a secretive animal and can be difficult to see in the wild. Caimans like to hide in weedy canals and in drains under roads and bridges in populated areas. They can only survive the winter if the temperature remains warm. That is why they are mainly found in south Florida. Caimans have been reported living in the Everglades. They have been breeding in the wild in Florida since the 1960s.

Unlike crocodiles, which dig nest holes in soil or mud, all alligators build mounds for their nests out of vegetation. The Spectacled Caiman also prepares a vegetation-based nest, where the female will lay 10 to 40 eggs each summer. The babies are preyed upon by birds, raccoons, and other animals. The adult Spectacled Caiman has no predators in Florida.

By advertising them as cute little baby

Spectacled Caimans are cute as babies but big as adults.

gators, the pet trade is able to sell lots of Spectacled Caimans. However, these animals are feisty and fierce. Even the babies will bite. Caimans need to be kept warm and will die quickly if they are exposed to freezing temperatures. They do not make good pets. Once full-grown, these large reptiles are too unruly for most pet owners to handle.

During breeding and nesting seasons, alligators are aggressive and may prove dangerous. Especially at risk for attack by these large reptiles are small dogs, cats, and children. Floridians have been seriously injured and even killed in alligator attacks.

Crocodiles tend to be less aggressive toward humans, but they should still be avoided in the wild. In fact, it is extremely unwise to try to feed or tame wild alligators or crocodiles. Once they are no longer afraid of humans, these reptiles will show aggression when they are seeking food.

In south Florida, Spectacled Caimans are seen as a nuisance exotic because their presence in suburban neighborhoods can be threatening. If you see *any kind* of alligator or crocodile in your yard, do not approach it. Stay indoors and keep your pets inside with you. Call the Florida Fish and Wildlife Conservation Commission's Nuisance Alligator hotline to report your sighting (see Resources on page 62 for contact information). They send out wildlife trappers to relocate or euthanize large reptiles on the loose.

Cane Toad *(Bufo marinus)*

Here in south Florida, animal clinics often must treat dogs with Cane Toad poisoning. This is because these huge toads are abundant now in more than 20 counties around the state.

The Cane Toad was first introduced to the state of Florida for the purpose of pest control. When insects were devastating the sugarcane

Amphibians

Lizards, snakes, turtles and alligators are all reptiles. These animals can be excellent swimmers, but they do not breathe underwater. They breathe the oxygen in air using lungs, like we do.

Amphibians lead two lives. As juveniles, they stay in the water, getting oxygen from water using gills. As they mature, amphibians develop lungs to breathe the air, and they leave the water for land. Adult amphibians can also breathe through their skin. They do not drink water, but take liquid into their bodies through their skin.

Amphibians include:

■ frogs and toads (over 5800 species)

■ newts and salamanders (over 500 species)

■ caecilians (legless tropical amphibians)

Frogs have smooth, wet skin, and they are good at hopping. Toads are drier, and their legs are shorter. Frogs will leap for food, grabbing prey with their long, sticky tongues. Males do the croaking, and a group of frogs is called a "chorus" because they will all croak together. Females lay hundreds of eggs at once in jellylike strings. The eggs hatch into tadpoles in a few days.

Amphibians are some of the world's oldest animals. They have been on Earth for as long as 360 million years. Yet many species of amphibians are in danger of extinction today. This is due to widespread overdevelopment, the draining of water for building purposes, and serious water pollution. Plus, invasions by exotics are contributing to a worldwide threat to the more vulnerable species of amphibians.

fields in the 1930s, these bug-eating toads were brought into the state and released. More Cane Toads were introduced to Florida's sugarcane fields in the 1940s, and again in the 1950s.

Cane Toad populations are expanding because the toads are breeding more than once a year. They breed in canals, ditches, shallow puddles, and pools. The female can produce 20,000 eggs! She lays her eggs in the shallow water, and they hatch as tadpoles soon after. Within a few months, the tadpoles grow into little toads.

Cane Toads like to be near water for reproduction, and they are attracted to asphalt and buildings for warmth. So these toads can be found all over suburban neighborhoods, on golf courses, and around school campuses and shopping malls. They especially love small man-made ponds, drain pipes, and gardens. Lights that attract insects will also attract Cane Toads. You can see them at night around your house lights or under streetlamps catching bugs.

Cane Toads are carnivores. They eat beetles, earwigs, ants, crickets, bees, and other insects. They will also eat snails, baby birds, small lizards, and snakes. They even prey on other, smaller toads and frogs. They love dog and cat food. If you feed your pets outside, these toads will eat right out of your pets' dishes. They may even dig around in your trash can for garbage and table scraps.

The male Cane Toads make a low-pitched trill in the springtime when it gets dark. On a night when there are a lot of toads trilling, boy, is it loud! When the Cane Toads sing, that's when you realize how many of them live in your neighborhood.

Some of the Cane Toads living in the wild in Florida were once pets that have escaped or were released by their owners. Surprisingly, this poisonous toad is sold by an enthusiastic pet trade. The toxins secreted by these toads can burn your skin and eyes, and it may make you ill. Since these toads are breeding like mad in the wild in Florida, the Cane Toad is not a pet that should be imported.

Although the Cane Toad was deliberately introduced to the state in the sugarcane fields, there are other reasons for the current overpopulation: the release of pet trade toads and the stowaways on cargo ships. Also, these huge toads have been able to dominate all of our native species of frogs and toads, consuming them and taking over their food and territory. However they arrive in Florida, once Cane Toads are here, they *rule*.

At this point, it would be impossible for Floridians to remove all the Cane Toads from our yards and neighborhoods. There are steps you can take as an individual, though, that might help keep them away. You can fence in your yard, making sure the fencing is embedded deep in the lawn so the toads can't crawl underneath. You can avoid feeding your pets outside to reduce the chances that these toads will come into your yard. Be sure not to leave any kind of food outside where they can find it. ***And never buy a Cane Toad as a pet.***

Cane Toads are the largest toads in the world, and a serious pest in areas where they are not native.

Florida's Other Exotic Amphibians

Except for some of the Cane Toads, most of the exotic amphibians on the loose in Florida were never pets. The non-native frogs and toads typically arrived here in cargo ships from other countries. Once cargo was unpacked around the state, the amphibians dispersed. Some were able to adapt to their new environment.

The tiny reddish-brown Greenhouse Frog *(Eleutherodactylus planirostris)* and the larger green and brown Cuban Treefrog *(Osteopilus septentrionalis)* are both native to Cuba and the Bahamas. Unlike the Cane Toad, a ground-dweller, these two web-footed frogs climb up trees and the sides of buildings.

Currently, both of these exotic frogs can be found all over Florida, from the Keys to the Panhandle. Scientists believe this wide scattering may be due to the popularity of imported plants shipped around the state. The frogs like to live in plant nurseries where tropical trees and shrubs are raised. When the plants are trucked to other areas of the state, the frogs hitchhike along.

Cuban Treefrogs have been seen in groups of 100 or more, clinging to the sides of buildings in Everglades National Park. These frogs grow to about five inches. They will eat practically anything they are able to swallow, including our disappearing native frogs and toads. Cuban Treefrogs are generalists, meaning they adapt better than other species. They are not as particular about what they eat or where they live. This allows them to outcompete Florida's native species for food and territory, making them an invasive species.

There is not much you can do to stop the invasion of non-native amphibians, since

The Greenhouse Frog hitchhikes to Florida in exotic plant cargo.

most are not released pets. Some scientists believe it is unwise for us to import exotic plant species because so often non-native animals and insects come hidden in this kind of cargo. In the warmth of Florida, many of the tropical species of invaders can survive and reproduce. Too often, these secret hitchhikers will cause problems once they start a new life in their adopted home.

Cuban Treefrogs secrete toxins that can burn your skin. They will lay 4000 eggs at a time, which is three times as many as our native frogs.

Killer Toads

My favorite kind of dog is the German Schnauzer. These small- to medium-sized hunting dogs remind me of old-fashioned psychiatrists with their bushy eyebrows and little gray beards. I've owned several Schnauzers in the course of my life. Right now, I share my home with two energetic Miniature German Schnauzers: Louie and Ralphie.

Several years ago, I had a Giant Schnauzer named Radar. He loved the outdoors and was always sniffing around in the trees and shrubs, looking for traces of animal life. All sorts of wildlife wanders through my yard, and Radar found this hard to resist. An exotic visitor, however, almost cost him his life.

The Cane Toad (*Bufo marinus*) is one of the world's largest toads, measuring 6 to 9 inches in length, not including the legs. It is not native to Florida. Rather, these huge toads are native to Central America, northern South America, and southern Texas along the Rio Grande River on the border of Mexico.

Toads are dry-skinned, bumpy-looking frogs. All species of toads have special glands that release toxins. These poisons help toads to kill their prey and defend themselves against attackers. The Cane Toad has an especially strong poison that can kill other animals, including dogs.

Of course, Radar was unaware of the facts about Cane Toads. So, when he spotted a giant toad near our swimming pool, he rushed in to get a closer look. I'm not sure who lunged first, but Cane Toads have been seen making attacks on threatening animals. First they puff up their bodies with air in order to appear larger. Then they tilt their heads downward to expose their poisonous glands. They can actually shoot their milky-white, foamy venom more than a foot! Once the toxin touches an animal's lips or mouth, the poison starts to burn. The animal backs off quickly, but the poison continues to have an effect.

When Radar stumbled into the house that day, he was foaming at the mouth. A smaller dog would have died from the poison, but Radar weighed 85 pounds. He was all muscle, and a fighter. Fortunately, too, I knew what to do.

I dragged Radar back outside and turned on the garden hose. Over and over for fifteen minutes, I flushed out his mouth with water. I made sure to keep his head pointed down so he didn't swallow. The toxins will speed up an animal's heart enough to cause heart failure, but watering down the poison can reduce the effect.

As soon as Radar stopped foaming, I drove him to the nearest veterinarian's office. We were lucky. Radar survived.

Cane Toads can be toxic to dogs.

Perhaps you can tell your parents about the problems associated with bringing exotic plants into our state. You might want to ask them to make sure your yard has native plants instead. Our native plants are easier to grow and require less water, so these species are better suited to Florida yards.

Red Lionfish (*Pterois volitans*)

Many of the exotic animals found in U.S. waters came from aquariums. Especially in the warm Florida waters, non-native fish and other animals are able to survive and breed.

Some Floridians who no longer want to care for their saltwater aquariums illegally dump their pets into the ocean. Many fish die this way. However, certain exotic species of fish, snails, and other aquarium pets adapt to life in the Florida coastal waters. They begin feeding and breeding there.

One species of saltwater aquarium fish that thrives in the wild in Florida is the Red Lionfish. Native to the Pacific and Indian oceans, this large fish is 11 to 15 inches long and weighs more than a pound. With its bright red and white stripes and needle-sharp spines, the fish is beautiful to look at but dangerous to touch. A member of the scorpionfish family, the Red Lionfish is poisonous.

These pretty fish are commonly sold for home and office-building aquariums. They are fun to watch, and most pet owners are unaware of the potential dangers.

The Red Lionfish is aggressive. When going after prey, the fish swim with spines pointed forward. They stalk crabs, shrimp, and smaller fish, which they will sting to paralyze and then swallow whole. In the Atlantic Ocean, this fish has no predators.

Venomous glands in the base of the fin spines of the Red Lionfish produce strong toxins. A sting can prove to be a serious health emergency. The pain is instant and intense, and may be followed by tingling, headache, vomiting, and heart problems. Sometimes people die from the sting of a Red Lionfish. Even

A favorite aquarium fish, the Red Lionfish is gorgeous and dangerous.

touching the dead body of this poisonous fish can cause blistering!

In recent years, the Red Lionfish has been reported off the coast of Palm Beach and Jacksonville. Reports of sightings have come from as far north as New York and as far south as the Caribbean islands. The numbers of Red Lionfish seen in the Atlantic have been increasing rapidly. This exotic fish appears to be expanding its territory and poses a threat to the Florida coastline.

In addition to being hazardous, the Red Lionfish is a hearty eater. This species is able to outcompete many other fish, and will consume the various types of fish that keep coral reefs clean and healthy. Since the Red Lionfish likes to live near coral reefs, this exotic species poses a threat. Our reefs are fragile and endangered, and the increased presence of this non-native species is adding to coral reef destruction.

If you see a Red Lionfish when you are swimming or snorkeling, report your sighting to the Florida Fish and Wildlife Conservation Commission on their wildlife hotline or, if you have photos, send them (see Resources on page 62 for contact information).

Be sure to swim in the opposite direction if you do see a Red Lionfish. And warn the people you are with to look but not touch.

Exotic Apple Snails

Every year, over 2000 species of exotic fish are brought to the U.S. for sale as aquarium pets. When aquarium owners move away or tire of their pet fish, however, they may dump the contents of the tank into local ponds, lakes, rivers, and canals. The Everglades has at least 15 species of exotic fish living there.

Abandoning aquarium pets is illegal, unfair to the fish, and damaging to the environment. Most of the aquarium pets will die in the wild, but some can survive and breed. In Florida, certain species of aquarium snails, called apple snails, have adapted to living in our fresh waters.

Apple snails are mollusks, which are soft-bodied animals with hard shells. Mollusks include snails, slugs, clams, mussels, oysters, and scallops. Currently, there are four species of non-native apple snails living and breeding in Florida. These species are native to South America. They pose a threat to Florida's only native apple snail.

The Florida Apple Snail (Pomacea paludosa) is the largest freshwater snail native to North America. This golf ball–sized snail lays round white eggs.

The species of apple snails used in aquariums can grow to the size of tennis balls. These exotic mollusks have been dumped in the wild all around the globe. Once released, these large snails have thrived in the warm, wet areas of the world where aquatic plants rise out of the water. This is where they lay their eggs. Exotic aquarium apple snails have colorful eggs of varied sizes.

In the wild in Florida, the exotic snails from aquariums have been increasing their populations since the 1990s. These large snails can produce up to 1000 eggs at a time, and the female will lay eggs continuously throughout the year.

Because of their size and rapid increase in numbers, the exotic apple snails are outcompeting the native Florida Apple Snail. The non-native snails consume all kinds of aquatic plants. In this way, they pose a threat to the Everglades and other wetland areas of the state.

To help fight the spread of non-native apple snails, Florida residents are encouraged to learn to identify exotic eggs. Whenever you see the brightly colored eggs on tree trunks or seawalls, docks or plant stems, scrape them into a zip-up plastic bag. Then freeze them to prevent hatching. **Never eat these toxic eggs!**

Obviously, you should **never dump an aquarium into Florida waters**. Instead, trade in unwanted fish and snails at your local pet store. Or donate them to a school, hospital, museum, or zoo. Maybe a friend will want to take your aquarium if you are done with it. As a last resort, a veterinarian will euthanize unwanted aquatic pets.

The colorful little eggs of exotic apple snails (on left) do not look the same as our native Florida Apple Snail's round white eggs (on right).

The Florida Apple Snail (on right) is much smaller than the exotic apple snails from aquariums (on left).

Chapter 5

Birds in Paradise

Sacred Ibis

In Florida, there are more exotic species of birds than any other kind of animal. Many are parrots of various types. In south Florida, where the winters are especially mild, 30 different species of parrots can be seen. You'll find them flying through the sky, squawking loudly, and chattering in large groups in trees and on telephone lines.

In fact, there may be a greater diversity of wild parrots living here than anywhere else in the world. This is because these different parrot species are from a variety of countries and were brought here as pets or are the offspring of former pets. Parrots and parakeets, conures and lovebirds, macaws, cockatoos and cockatiels are all sold by the pet trade, and have all been released by their owners. None of the parrot species we see in the wild are native to Florida.

Parrots have predators in Florida, including large lizards and snakes, cats, raccoons, and other mammals. These birds also die from ingesting pesticides, fertilizers, and other poisonous chemicals in yards and parks and on crops. Habitat loss due to the overdevelopment of our state means that parrots must constantly search for new nesting sites.

Conures and other parakeets are small parrots native to Central and South America. Brightly colored and affectionate, conures and parakeets of different species have been imported by the U.S. pet trade for more than 100 years. In Florida, escaped or released conures and parakeets can survive rather easily in our warm environment with our year-round supply of vegetation.

The colorful little Australian Budgerigar is commonly sold in pet stores as a "parakeet."

The most common pet-store parrot is the colorful little "budgie" or Budgerigar (*Melopsittacus undulatus*). These cute parakeets are native to Australia. They have been reported to be breeding in the wild in some of Florida's larger cities, especially along the Gulf Coast.

Red-Crowned Amazon
(*Amazona viridigenalis*)

These beautiful parrots are native to the east coast of Mexico. They are usually 11 to 13 inches in height, with stocky bodies and square tails. Bright green in color, they have red feathers on their heads and faces, and blue streaks behind their eyes. Their bills are yellow. In Mexico, the Red-Crowned Amazon is endangered due to habitat loss and the capture of so many of these incredible birds for sale as pets. The native population of this species has been estimated at less than 2000 birds.

The beautiful Red-Crowned Amazon is one of the most common species of exotic parrots found on the loose in south Florida.

In the U.S., these exotic parrots can be seen flying around in large flocks in California and Florida. If raised by humans, they can be affectionate and playful. For this reason, these parrots are popular in the pet trade, where they are usually called Green-Cheeked Parrots. (Their cheek feathers are a light green color.) They were one of the first parrot species reported breeding in the wild in Florida. Since the 1970s, these parrots have

Paulie

One hot afternoon, I was called by a young family who had discovered a Red-Crowned Amazon sitting in a tree in their yard. The parrot seemed calm and curious as I approached. He examined my face with his wise yellow eyes. When I held out my monkey net, he fluffed his feathers. Instead of taking flight, he seemed to shrug his shoulders as if to say, "So okay, take me home already."

My back patio is screened, and I keep a few large cages out there for occasional overnight guests. Paulie, as I called him, settled in at once, munching on a snack of sliced fruit. He watched me with his golden eyes. "Hello," he would say, "how are you?" His voice was eerily female, like that of a sweet old woman.

When parrots speak like this, they are imitating, not conversing. Researchers who work with talking birds report that a small percentage of the birds can understand the meaning of the words they speak. For example, studies have shown that certain birds can identify in words the colors of items they pick up with their bills. This is rare, however, and indicates an especially high level of intelligence.

In the middle of the night, I awoke to the cries of an elderly woman. "Help," she screamed. "Help me."

I jumped out of bed and, with my husband two steps behind, rushed to the back of the house. Was it our next-door neighbor, an older woman who lived alone? Was she out in our backyard, in some kind of trouble?

My husband flipped on a floodlight, illuminating the backyard. A large raccoon stood just outside our screened patio, frozen in the sudden glare.

"Help me," begged Paulie in his old lady voice. His beady eyes were frightened. He knew this predator could try to hurt him.

I clapped my hands and shouted at the raccoon, and it darted off into the darkness. Paulie ruffled his feathers and we locked eyes. I could see the relief reflected there.

Paulie lives at a local bird sanctuary now. He seems happy there. The owners have told me that he is a talking wonder, the most intelligent parrot they have ever taken in. His vocabulary is huge, his personality charming. Visitors love him.

It seems obvious Paulie prefers a life in captivity. I would guess that he was the beloved pet of an aged woman who either died or moved away. Some abandoned parrots adapt to living in the wild. Others, however, die when left to fend for themselves. This is especially true for older birds that have lived many years as cherished pets.

Paulie was smart enough to ask for the help he needed to survive. Most animals cannot do this, so it is up to us to make the effort required to protect them from abuse and extinction.

been seen on the loose here. They are one of the most common wild parrot species in our state.

The Red-Crowned Amazon is considered an agricultural pest. This is because they travel in large flocks that eat lots of fruits, berries, flowers, and pine seeds. Like all parrots, they nest in tree hollows. They will take over the holes made in the trunks of trees by woodpeckers, owls, and other native birds, leaving them without a home.

There is no denying it—the Red-Crowned Amazon is a very loud bird. A flock flying overhead will constantly squawk as the birds move between feeding areas. When captive, these birds can become quite skilled at mimicking the sounds around them. They will make the sound of a telephone ringing, a vacuum cleaner or dishwasher in operation, a person coughing, or a dog barking. Some can be trained to talk.

Monk Parakeet
(Myiopsitta monachus)

The most common parrot on the loose in Florida is the Monk Parakeet. This colorful bird is also called the Quaker Parakeet. That's because gray feathers on the face, throat, and breast make this bird look as if it is wearing the old-fashioned costume of a religious Quaker. The Monk Parakeet is a bright green parrot with an orange bill. It is typically just under a foot tall.

These parrots travel in large flocks. They squawk loudly as they fly from palm tree to phone line to oak tree in search of food. They eat grass, wildflowers, weeds, plants, grass seed, and insects. You can attract them into your backyard with a hanging feeder filled with wild bird seed.

A 1960s pet fad ended with the release and abandonment of Monk Parakeets. Today, these loud birds can be seen in trees and on telephone wires all over Florida.

Monk Parakeets are the most friendly wild parrot species in Florida. They are all former pets and the offspring of pets, so many are familiar with people. When rescued, they may adapt to living in a home or aviary and will bond with caring humans.

In the wild, the Monk Parakeet lives in large groups called colonies. These birds have the unique ability to weave huge stick nests from twigs and flexible branches on trees. The entire colony of parrots will live and breed together in the giant stick nest they build as a team. These nests can be as big as a car! The parrots actually create separate entrances to the nest for each pair of breeding birds. The Monk Parakeet is the only species of parrot that does not nest in a tree hollow.

Monk Parakeets from the international pet trade are now living in the wild in Spain, Israel, Puerto Rico, Bermuda, and Japan. In the 1960s, many of these parrots were brought into the U.S., where they were popular pets. By the 1970s, they were reported breeding in the wild in 30 states. These days there are large colonies living in New York City, Chicago, San Francisco, and in many city parks around the country. Here in Florida, there may be more than 100,000 Monk Parakeets living in at least 50 counties around the state.

These parrots are highly social. They are friendly, playful, and can be excellent talkers. Some will develop large vocabularies. Monk Parakeets make good pets. In captivity, they can live to be 30 years old.

However, Monk Parakeets are extremely loud. Their squawking is constant and high-pitched throughout the daytime. They will gnaw and chew on lots of items, including things they should not eat. They are messy and will occasionally bite the hand that feeds them. All too often, these wonderful birds are abandoned by owners who can no longer care for them.

Socialization is important to these parrots. They need to be with their own species. But it can be difficult for a hand-raised or long-term pet parrot to adapt to life in the wild. Colonies do not always allow newcomers from cages to join the group. Pet owners should never release their parrots, which is an illegal act in Florida. In some states, it is no longer legal to import, sell, or own Monk Parakeets either.

These parrots are regarded as agricultural pests in Brazil and other South American countries where they are native. The more than 100 members in a flock can swoop in and devour entire crops. Their giant stick nests are often built in undesirable places, such as on top of electric transformers, streetlights, and telephone poles. Sometimes power blackouts are blamed on these birds.

In south Florida, Monk Parakeets often build their stick nests on top of the platforms for the tall light poles that light up playing fields and parks. This is seen as a nuisance, so the electric company will destroy the nests. Sometimes baby birds will be forced to leave their nests before they are ready.

You can help these amazing parrots by allowing them to build nests in your yard. If you set out hanging bird feeders filled with wild bird seed, they may come to eat and decide to stay. Monk Parakeets are curious and fearless, so you may be able to befriend them if you are patient and attentive. Be sure to keep your pet cat inside the house. And ask your parents not to use pesticides on the lawn.

Muscovy Duck *(Cairina moschata)*

Before the iguana invasion, the Muscovy Duck was Florida's least favorite exotic animal. These non-migratory ducks are native to Mexico and to Central and South America. However, they have been reported living and breeding in Florida since 1967. They can be found now in almost every county in the state. Muscovy Ducks can also be found in other states, where they live in parks and on lakes.

The Muscovy Duck has a full body and a bright red face mask.

In their native countries, the wild Muscovy is a lean duck with lots of predators. When bred on farms, however, the species is fatter and meatier. Females weigh 6 to 8 pounds or more, and males may weigh up to 15 pounds. The plumper variety of Muscovy was brought into the U.S. to live on farms. Many ducks escaped or were released. Over the years, these ducks have reproduced rapidly and much too successfully.

The female Muscovy may breed 3 times a year, and she lays 10 to 20 eggs per "clutch." Many of the young ducks do not survive since they are preyed upon by turtles, alligators, wading birds such as herons, and hawks. However, the ducks that reach their full adult size have few predators in Florida.

The Muscovy is adorable as a baby duckling, sort of cute as a juvenile, and downright ugly as an adult. When fully grown, these glossy ducks have dark brown or black bodies with white head and tail feathers. They have bright red, bumpy-looking faces. The red face mask is called "caruncling." The females typically have more white feathers on their heads and necks than males do. The males have more red on the face and a feather crest on the top of the head.

In a kind of reverse ugly duckling story, these ducks are often fed and admired until they are fully grown. Suddenly, nobody wants them around anymore. Hand-fed baby birds become familiar with humans and used to receiving food from them. Once ignored, the abandoned ducks can turn aggressive. They will hang around the homes and city buildings where they were fed as ducklings, sometimes in large hungry groups. Their droppings are messy and can be found all over—on sidewalks, driveways, parking lots, pool decks, and docks.

In the wild, these ducks will eat plants, grass, seeds, small reptiles, fish, and insects. Human handouts they will eat include bread, french fries, and dog or cat food. An improper diet like this can cause "angel wing." This is a condition in which the duck's wings stick out from its body.

If people insist on feeding Muscovy Ducks, they should choose food suitable for the species. On the farms where domestic ducks are raised, they are fed specially-made duck food or "mash" with cracked corn, vegetable trimmings, worms, and other protein foods. The ducks are fed near or in the water where

Muscovy Ducks overpopulate lakes and parks throughout the state.

they live, rather than on the street or sidewalk where they do not belong.

The number of Muscovy Ducks living and breeding on the loose in Florida continues to grow. These big ducks are competing with our smaller native waterfowl (birds that, like ducks, are often in the water) for food and territory. Muscovy Ducks have been reported breeding with native species of ducks, creating hybrid species.

The media sometimes reports mass killings of Muscovy Ducks by home or business owners tired of chasing the birds off their properties. This is an illegal act because all animals in our state, both native and exotic, are protected by animal cruelty laws. However, with the simple step of local population control, you may be able to help reduce the Muscovy Duck overpopulation problem. And that would then prevent the heartless slaughter of this unpopular exotic animal.

What You Can Do

The best care we can provide for the many Muscovy Ducks living near the ponds, lakes, rivers, and canals in our state is population control. This is something you can help with near your own home.

Start by observing the Muscovy Ducks in your neighborhood to find out where they make their nests. These ducks will dig shallow holes in tucked-away spots. Usually these spots are not too far from the body of water where they will teach their babies to swim.

Typically, the female will lay one egg in her nest each day until she has completed her clutch, or set of eggs. Then she will pluck out her own feathers to line her nest and begin incubation. The mother duck sits on her eggs for around 3 weeks or until they hatch.

Before she finishes laying all her eggs, however, the mother duck will come and go. When she does, she will leave her nest unguarded. Here's where you can participate. During the first week after the eggs are laid, the egg yolks have not yet developed into chicks. If you remove most of the clutch—but not all the eggs—the mother duck will not move on to a new nest and reclutch. She will sit on the remaining eggs until they hatch. If you take all her eggs, she will start over, laying a whole new clutch in a better hiding spot.

So, you should remove all but 2 or 3 eggs while the female is away from the nest. Since they have so many predators as ducklings, not all of the babies that do hatch will survive. In this way, you can help to reduce the population for the next generation of Muscovy Ducks in your neighborhood.

Put the eggs you remove from the nest into a zip-up plastic bag. Then put the bag in your home freezer for 24 hours. If you toss the eggs into a garbage can without freezing them first, they may hatch. The warmth of the can may allow the eggs to continue to develop. This happens sometimes, resulting in orphan ducklings.

Be careful not to approach the mother duck when she is sitting on her nest or caring for her newly hatched babies. She will hiss, lunge, and snap to protect her young. The bite of a Muscovy Duck can hurt. If the mother duck becomes too frightened, she may fly off, abandoning her babies. Orphan ducklings do not usually survive on their own.

Other Exotic Waterfowl

Neighborhoods or cities import non-native ducks, geese, and swans. They do this to "decorate" ponds and lakes, golf courses and country clubs, urban and suburban developments, places where animals are seen as nothing more than attractive displays.

When the exotic waterfowl require more food or territory for breeding and nesting, the birds will fly away. They will look for bodies of fresh water where they can find what they need. The birds that survive and breed in Florida by adapting to the environment may cause problems.

The exotic waterfowl species tend to be large birds that compete with our native waterfowl for food and territory. They eat plants that grow in the water and other native vegetation. Sometimes they trample the nests of smaller water birds. Once they reach adult size, these non-native birds have few predators in Florida.

At this time, most of the exotic waterfowl species in Florida are not considered nuisance animals or invasive pests. Many are pretty birds,

Because of their beauty, swans are used to "decorate" private lakes and ponds.

Non-native geese can be found in parks and on lakes in Florida.

and they usually avoid the hostile reactions Muscovy Ducks receive. However, none of these birds are native to this area. They are imported by humans unaware of their potential threat to our fragile ecosystem.

It is sad to see lovely birds like swans confined to indoor pools in hotels and tiny man-made lakes on golf courses. It is cruel to regard certain kinds of birds as nothing but decorations. After all, animals are *not* alive simply to amuse and entertain us. In a perfect world, humans would treat all animals with the respect that every species deserves.

More Problem Birds

On a regular basis, new species of non-native birds are found to be breeding in Florida. Many are escaped pets.

The Common Myna (*Acridotheres tristis*) from southeast Asia now lives in some cities in south and central Florida. You can spot them around fast-food parking lots, where they like to eat garbage.

The first few brightly colored Purple Swamphens (*Porphyrio porphyrio*) escaped from their owner's yard in south Florida in the 1990s. This Eurasian bird reproduces at a high rate, and now it is expanding its range. This means Purple Swamphens can be found in more and more places, where they may eat other birds' eggs and nestlings.

The Sacred Ibis (*Threskiornis aethiopicus*) is a species of wading bird from Africa. These majestic birds have been nesting in the Everglades since 2007.

There are just too many exotic bird species on the loose in Florida.

Chapter 6
Pets Gone Wild

Rhesus Monkey (baby)

Vervet Monkey
(Chlorocebus aethiops)

Groups, or "troops," of Vervet Monkeys have been on the loose in the Fort Lauderdale area since the 1950s. The population of these African monkeys is expanding. The original monkeys belonged to a tourist attraction. However, the animals either escaped or, more likely, were abandoned when the owner closed the business.

Vervets are lovely silvery-gray monkeys with sweet black faces topped by a band of bright white fur. They have black ears, hands, feet, and tail tips. The Vervet is a medium-size monkey. These animals are between 1 and 2 feet tall, and they weigh 5 to 17 pounds. They eat leaves, plants, flowers, fruits, and insects. Birds' eggs and baby birds are also tempting to these monkeys.

Vervets travel in troops of 10 to 50 monkeys. All are good climbers, jumpers, and swimmers. They will invade crops and steal human food, so they can easily become pests.

Rhesus Monkey (Macaca mulatta)

Another monkey reported living and breeding in several counties—especially the Fort Lauderdale area in Broward County—is the Rhesus Monkey. Also called Rhesus Macaques or simply "macaques," these large, noisy monkeys are native to Asia. They are brownish-gray with pink faces and rears.

Rhesus Monkeys eat fruit, seeds, leaves, insects, and small animals. Troops can grow to more than 100 monkeys. They will move into cities and learn to rely on humans for hand-

Vervet Monkeys like to live in wooded areas near streams, rivers, and lakes.

Monkey See

One summer day not long ago, I received a call from a woman living in an apartment complex north of Fort Lauderdale. She told me about a little monkey she had seen climbing on the apartment buildings, swinging from patio to patio. "It must be somebody's lost pet, the poor thing," she said.

Monkeys on the loose are almost impossible to capture. That is, unless they wish to be captured. Most do not. Monkeys are wild animals and, although they can be trained, do not make good pets.

As I drove my van south on the interstate, I pictured the monkey hanging from high-rise porch railings as if they were rainforest tree branches. I find it strange and troubling that several species of monkeys are living and breeding on their own in Florida.

When I arrived at the apartment complex, the woman who had called me waved from her patio. She pointed to the flat roof of a tall building that overlooked the complex's swimming pool. I could see a tiny monkey running on all fours along the edge of the roof.

The situation did not look promising. The monkey was five stories above the ground and it seemed quick and independent. When I called to it by whistling and chirping, it did not respond. I knew there was very little chance I'd be able to capture the animal.

My choices were to either shoot the monkey with a tranquilizer gun or let it go. If hit with the tranquilizer, the monkey might fall off the roof. Also, such drugs do not take effect immediately. The monkey might run away and hide while still awake. Later, the animal could be hurt or killed while lying unconscious in its hiding spot.

So I opted to let the monkey go. But first I told a friend of mine, a local wildlife trapper who specializes in primates. My friend promised to spend time at the apartment complex to see if he might be able to capture the monkey when it was on the ground. Since there are a number of monkeys that roam freely in south Florida, my friend receives lots of calls like the one I responded to that day.

outs. This is not desirable since these monkeys carry diseases.

Rhesus Monkeys are highly adaptable in captivity. For this reason, they are often used in medical experiments. These monkeys are so intelligent they were sent into space as America's first astronauts!

Until a few years ago, a private medical company was raising thousands of Rhesus Monkeys in the Florida Keys. The monkeys overcrowded the mangrove trees that lined the shoreline. They also eroded the beach and polluted the water. Public complaints resulted

Rhesus Monkeys are often used by research laboratories and can carry dangerous diseases.

Monkey Business

Releasing monkeys of any species in parks and wooded lots is an illegal act. Unfortunately, even animal welfare and animal cruelty laws do not stop some people from abandoning their unwanted animals.

Owners of traveling animal displays, petting zoos, and roadside attractions sometimes find it difficult to sell off their old and unwanted monkeys. Some will pretend to have the best interest of the animals at heart. They'll choose a place like Florida, with our mild winter climate, and then travel here to dump their monkeys. These lawbreakers have added to our booming exotic animal populations.

Monkeys are incredibly smart and cute as babies, but they begin to behave aggressively at the age of 3 or 4. This is when some irresponsible owners dump their pets in the wild. Monkeys will scratch and bite, and some carry serious diseases.

Macaques have become popular pets in the Miami area. These monkeys are former lab animals and their offspring. Unfortunately, most pet buyers don't know that many macaques carry a virus that can kill humans. Since the virus does not make the monkey ill, very few pet owners are aware of the dangers of owning this exotic animal.

Exotic mammals can be especially dangerous to us because, as mammals, we are vulnerable to the diseases they carry. Monkeys do not belong inside our homes. They should be living in the open areas and rainforests of their native countries. Certain European nations no longer allow people to own monkeys and other wild animals that may infect humans with their diseases.

If you see a monkey on the loose in your neighborhood, report your sighting to a humane trapper. Never try to capture the monkey on your own. Monkeys are wild animals and they will bite.

---

in legal action to force the medical research firm to remove the monkeys from the islands.

Several troops of Rhesus Monkeys have been living in central Florida along the Silver River since the 1930s. They were originally released by a tourist attraction. These monkeys hide in the dense trees, where they continue to breed. They will behave aggressively if approached by people.

Squirrel Monkey (Saimiri sciureus)

The tiny South American Squirrel Monkey has been reported breeding in several counties around the state. These cute little monkeys can be seen on occasion in parks and neighborhoods in the Fort Lauderdale area.

Squirrel Monkeys have been on the loose in our state since the 1960s. They originally escaped from or were abandoned by tourist attractions and small zoos. As rainforest animals, these little guys are excellent climbers and jumpers. They are only 10 inches tall and weigh less than 2 pounds. Squirrel Monkeys have short brown fur with orange coloring on their backs and limbs. Their faces are black with a white mask around the eyes.

Squirrel Monkeys eat fruits, seeds, nuts, insects, and other small animals. They will eat

Squirrel Monkeys are popular pets until they reach adulthood. The species is sometimes used in medical experiments.

birds' eggs and young birds. In the wild, these loud monkeys travel in troops of 500 or more! They chirp and peep, and bark when angry.

Feral Cat *(Felis catus)*

One of the most problematic pets on the loose in Florida is the domestic cat. The estimated 10 million feral cats in our state pose a major threat to native wildlife. They kill hundreds of millions of small animals every year.

Modern-day pet cats are the descendants of the wild cats of Africa and Asia. The Egyptians first domesticated these cats, or tamed them, about 4000 years ago. In this country, pet cats are exotics. They were brought to the U.S. by early colonists.

Any domesticated animal that returns to the wild, living outside and fending for itself, will develop certain behaviors that may threaten the environment. In fact, all feral animals can become invasive species. This is because they have not evolved in the habitats in which they are living. They are not a natural part of the habitat. These non-natives compete with native animals for food and shelter. They destroy habitat and hunt the native wildlife. Often, the feral invaders have high reproduction rates and few predators, so their populations increase rapidly.

Feral cats are currently on the loose in nearly every county in Florida. They are able to breed successfully and are comfortable in the wild throughout our mild winters. These cats can outcompete many native animals for food. They also prey on native species of small reptiles, amphibians, mammals, and birds.

It is the cat's natural instinct to hunt anything that moves and to kill the prey even if it is not hungry. In Florida, feral cats are killing lizards, snakes, rabbits, mice, and birds. A single cat in the wild in Florida may kill 100 or more smaller animals each year.

All over the world, cats are especially damaging to native bird populations. On certain islands, the feral cats have wiped out entire species of small birds. The cat will capture young birds when they first leave the nest to spend time on the ground.

Feral cats serve as a serious threat to Burrowing Owls because these birds are easy prey. That's because they live on the ground in the holes they dig. In Florida, these tiny owls are of special concern because the overdevelopment of our state is destroying so much of their native habitat. Feral cats are reducing their populations even more.

Feral cats live in colonies near the beach around the state, where they prey on our endangered sea turtle hatchlings. Certain species of beach mice are also endangered, and feral cats are part of the reason for their population reductions.

Feral cats are either former pets or the offspring of abandoned pets that were never spayed or neutered to prevent breeding. The root of the problem with feral cats is not this animal's natural instinct for hunting. Rather, it is our lack of responsibility in caring for our pet cats properly.

Feral cats are homeless domestic pets surviving in the wild. There may be more feral cats than domestic cats living in Florida.

If you don't want to become part of the problem, you can follow a few simple rules regarding cats:

- Keep your pet cats inside day and night.
- Bring pet food inside at night.
- Keep birdfeeders in the open so cats cannot hide to prey on birds while they are eating.
- Do not feed feral cats unless you plan to adopt them.
- Spay or neuter all adopted cats.

If you adopt a cat, make a commitment to caring for your pet for its lifetime. If you are moving or can no longer take care of your pet, be sure to find a new home for it. **Never abandon your cat in the wild**.

Wild Pigs

There are an estimated 500,000 feral pigs living in the state of Florida. Only Texas has more pigs on the loose. In our state, these huge mammals have been reported breeding in the wild in almost every county.

The Spanish explorers who settled in Florida in the 1500s brought along their native domesticated pigs. The Native Americans living in Florida learned to raise these intelligent animals too. Many pigs escaped into the wild. They have been on the loose ever since, reproducing quickly and successfully.

Wild pigs can weigh more than 200 pounds. They have big, sharp tusks. These mammals carry a number of diseases that can prove dangerous to humans.

Wild pigs like to live in forested areas with lots of acorns, their favorite food. They need to live near shallow water where they can roll around to keep cool. In Florida, the full-grown adults have few predators. However, alligators, black bears, and panthers will prey on feral pigs.

Wild pigs are pests. They travel in groups called "sounders" to invade farmland, devouring both crops and livestock feed. They prey on native animals, especially species that nest on the ground, such as sea turtles. The feral pigs outcompete our native animals for food and territory. They are adaptable and will eat many kinds of foods in huge amounts. They even eat tree seeds and seedlings, which damages forests.

Occasionally, pet Pot-Bellied Pigs escape or are abandoned in the wild in Florida. These domesticated pigs are imported from Vietnam by the pet trade. Pot-Bellied Pigs are affectionate and playful, like pet dogs. However, they

The 14 species of Pot-Bellied Pigs may be advertised by the pet trade as small pets, but adults can weigh 100 to 300 pounds.

can weigh more than 300 pounds and are destructive and aggressive when seeking food. Animal shelters are overflowing with unwanted Pot-Bellied Pigs.

In the state of Florida, it is legal to hunt wild pigs. This includes escaped pets. People tend to be hostile toward these animals because they are widely regarded as destructive pests. So it is not a good idea to keep a pig as a pet in Florida.

More Problem Pets

Prairie dogs are native to the western states, but not to Florida. During the 1970s, these small rodents suddenly became popular pets. Once the fad ended, many were released into the wild.

Prairie dogs belong to the squirrel family. They are important to the ecosystems of their native grasslands in Canada, northern Mexico, and the states west of the Mississippi River.

They serve as prey to many different animals, and their constant digging helps to keep the soil healthy.

These animals are very social and live in large groups in underground burrows. Their huge colonies are called "towns." Burrows may

Prairie Dogs eat plants and insects. They live in burrows. When excited, they bark like a dog.

have tunnels that stretch up to 16 feet deep and 100 feet long.

As pets, prairie dogs may adapt to humans and act affectionately. However, these animals have periods of aggressive behavior. In general, prairie dogs are unhappy living in captivity, especially without other prairie dogs for company. They need to run free and, in an enclosed environment, they will scamper about constantly as if looking to get out.

In late 1995, five cases of plague in humans were reported. Each case was linked to prairie dog pets. The plague was carried by fleas on the prairie dogs. A few years later, pet owners became ill with a potentially fatal disease called tularemia. It was caused by a bacteria associated with prairie dogs. Finally, in 2003 pet-store prairie dogs were infected with monkeypox. This is a rare African virus that causes serious illness in humans. All trade and sales of prairie dogs were banned in the U.S. and Europe.

In September 2008, the U.S. ban on prairie dogs was lifted. Therefore, these animals are once again for sale as pets in most states. Recently, a teacher in Palm Beach County was bitten by a prairie dog burrowing on school grounds.

Hedgehogs are small spiny mammals native to Europe, Asia, and Africa. They are not native to the U.S., but are popular with the international pet trade. In Florida, they are occasionally seen in the wild.

Hedgehogs are nocturnal animals. They sleep all day and bustle about at night. They grunt and snuffle, and their pointy noses resemble a pig's snout. They usually weigh less than two pounds and are a foot or so long.

Hedgehogs have brown or tan fur with stiff, hollow hairs that stick out like spikes.

There are more than a dozen species of hedgehogs. All have cute little raccoon faces and beady black eyes.

These spines are not poisonous or barbed, but they are sharp. To protect itself, the hedgehog rolls up into a spiny ball. In Florida, owls and other birds will prey on hedgehogs.

In the wild, hedgehogs consume lots of insects. They eat snails, frogs and toads, small snakes, mice, birds, and birds' eggs. Hedgehogs live in burrows they dig in the ground. They require a warm climate to survive if they have been raised as pets.

In captivity, however, these quiet animals do not always adapt well. They do not like enclosed environments and may not cope well with dramatic temperature changes. Feeding hedgehogs an improper diet, such as cat or dog food, can lead to an early death for them. They love sweets but will become overweight and sickly on such a diet.

Hedgehogs were introduced to New Zealand for pest control purposes. However, they have caused their own environmental problems. This includes damage to native plants, snails, and ground-nesting birds. Here in Florida, our ecosystem faces similar threats from these animals.

The Gambian Pouch Rat (Cricetomys gambianus) is one of the world's largest rats. This long-tailed African rodent can grow to the size of a small raccoon and weigh up to 9 pounds. The pouch rat is related to hamsters and gerbils. Like its relatives, this rodent is nocturnal and has a food storage pouch in each cheek.

For a few years the sale of these rodents was banned due to outbreaks of monkeypox. Now the giant pet rats are breeding on at least one of the islands south of Miami.

Between 2000 and 2002, a pet owner released 6 or 7 Gambian Pouch Rats on the island of Grassy Key. This illegal act has led to the establishment of the first known breeding population in the U.S. Biologists warn that, if these rats reach the mainland and invade the Everglades, ecological damage may occur. After all, they are quite large and eat a wide variety of fruits, vegetables, snails, insects, nuts, and seeds. That means these rats will be able to outcompete our native species for food and territory. Plus, they carry diseases that pose risks to humans.

If you ever see a prairie dog, hedgehog, or Gambian Pouch Rat on the loose, do not try to capture it yourself. You can call a local humane trapper. Also, report your sighting to a wildlife rescue center or the Florida Fish and Wildlife Conservation Commission wildlife hotline (see Resources on page 62).

The Gambian Pouch Rat, also known as the Giant African Pouched Rat, is sold by the pet trade. Buyers who like hamsters and gerbils may not realize how large this African rodent can become.

Protecting Our Animals

Wild animals do not make good pets. They can become aggressive and may transmit diseases to humans. It is difficult to feed them properly, and care may become expensive and problematic as the animal reaches adult size.

A life in captivity is not good for wild animals. Most are uncomfortable in confinement and do not receive a natural diet or enough sunlight. Imported animals may have trouble adjusting to a new climate, one that may not be appropriate for the species. Since most pet owners cannot give their animals all of their attention, wild pets are usually caged and alone all day with little or no amusement. Life is dull, lonely, and unnatural for a captive animal.

Wild animals should remain in the wild with members of their own species. In their natural habitats, wild animals fit specific ecosystems, helping to maintain environmental balance. Living and breeding in their own territories, wild animals keep nature in balance. They are not on this planet so that we can selfishly destroy their habitats and abduct them for our own entertainment.

The international pet trade is a massive industry that brings in a lot money. According to the U.S. Fish and Wildlife Service, more than 200 million birds, fish, and other exotic wildlife are imported into the country legally each year. Many more exotics are smuggled in from other countries illegally. The exotic pet trade does not have government oversight. Yet, the industry has more than doubled in size over the last two decades.

Pet dealers and breeders rely on a never-ending supply of new animals to sell. As people tire of familiar pets, new species are introduced by the pet industry. Whenever pets lose popularity, the animals are released in parks and woods around the U.S.

This system of irresponsibility is not good for our native animals. It is also unfair to the abandoned pets. Many die, while others become nuisance exotics that annoy the public.

Florida has a very active wildlife pet industry. There are many wild-pet stores, wild-animal breeders, traveling zoos and exhibitions, and private exotic-animal collections. Fortunately, Florida also has some of the strictest laws in the country regarding ownership of wildlife.

During the 1970s, attacks by pet "big cats" (like cheetahs and ocelots) around the state led to the establishment of laws in Florida that required people to have a license to own large, dangerous exotic animals. More recently, the Florida Fish and Wildlife Conservation Commission enacted new rules for the ownership of certain species of exotic reptiles. Owners of pythons, anacondas, and Nile Monitor lizards now must have special permits. Microchips are implanted in the registered animals to help identify their owners if the pets are ever found loose.

In 2007, the state of Florida began to regulate ownership of Red-Eared Slider Turtles. By 2008, breeding this species of turtle was outlawed in our state.

Ownership of macaque monkeys, caimans, and certain other non-native animals also requires permits here in Florida. You can check the state regulations regarding exotic pets on the Florida Fish and Wildlife Conservation Commission website, which is listed in the Resources section (see page 62).

Our Endangered Species

The Florida Fish and Wildlife Conservation Commission publishes a list of animals and plants facing extinction in our state. The American Crocodile is on the Florida endangered species list. So is the Key Largo Woodrat. The Eastern Indigo Snake and the Gopher Tortoise are on the state's threatened species list. That means they are not quite endangered yet, but getting close. Because it may one day be endangered too, the Burrowing Owl appears on the state list of species of special concern.

Under the Endangered Species Act, it is illegal to import, export, or sell listed animals from state to state. It is against the law to kill any of these animals without a special permit. The law forbids bothering and harassing the species on the lists. Trapping or taking in these animals is restricted to those with the proper permits.

Until the last few centuries, species became extinct through natural causes such as climate change or natural disasters. Now, *most extinctions are due to human activities.* The major threats to our vulnerable animal species these days are habitat loss, wildlife hunting, trapping by the pet trade, and the introduction of non-native species.

Of all the species that ever lived on this earth, 99 percent are currently extinct. The wave of extinction that is occurring now is bigger and quicker than ever before. This is because humans are spreading the problem around the globe. Only in the last few thousand years of our planet's history have humans been disturbing habitat by clearing forests, draining marshes, filling in swamps, planting crops, irrigating dry land, building cities and towns, increasing manmade fires, and killing off natural predators. Only in recent history have modern humans been traveling the world for trade and war, bringing along animals and plants of various species. *We humans are actually super-invaders—the most dangerous exotic of all!*

Fortunately, we may be capable of serving as helpful rather than nuisance exotics. It is not too late for us to save the species we are endangering.

The U.S. government and various private organizations have established wildlife refuges, national and state parks and sanctuaries, and nature preserves. All of these places are meant to help protect our endangered species in the habitats they need to live in to survive. It may still be possible to save more of our natural ecosystems and demonstrate that we value other species. Florida needs a new development plan that would set aside additional parcels of natural habitat. We need a statewide campaign to return land that has not been developed to natural habitat.

All animals living in the state of Florida are protected by animal cruelty laws. Migratory birds are protected under special federal laws to prevent people from killing or trapping them. Endangered animals are also protected by special regulations.

What You Can Do

There are things you can do to help protect Florida's land and wildlife:

- Write to your state legislators about the need to preserve our natural habitat.
- Volunteer to help out at a local wildlife refuge or park.
- Volunteer to assist in community cleanups or planting events to help preserve local habitat.
- Help your family plant native trees, shrubs, and flowers in your yard for animal habitat.
- When hiking, stay on the trails to avoid disrupting wildlife.
- Conserve water and energy to help preserve Florida's resources and the species we share them with.
- Never buy wild animals, including exotic species.
- Write to the Florida Fish and Wildlife Conservation Commission and urge them to *ban the sale of iguanas and other exotic pets* in our state (see Resources on page 62 for contact information).
- *Never abandon your pets in the wild.*

It is impossible to get rid of all the exotic species in Florida. This includes non-native plant invaders, insects, and animals.

Chapter 7
Exotic Florida

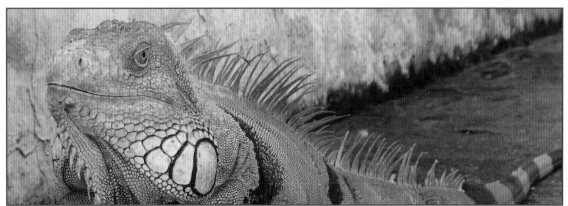

Green Iguana

Florida is a beautiful place blessed with unique landscapes, a tropical sort of climate, and lush vegetation. Our state has different habitats that appeal to different species. There are coastal beaches, tall pine forests, mangrove swamps, wetland marshes, and coral reefs. Florida is the only state in the continental U.S. with coral reefs. Only Florida is home to the magnificent wetlands called the Everglades.

We also have massive disturbances in the environment. These are caused by the draining of the wetlands for farmland and the building of homes. Widespread overdevelopment clears the land of forest, disturbs the soil, degrades and destroys natural habitats. These changes are bad for native animals, and good for the exotics. The modern Florida landscape no longer supports all of our native fauna, yet it attracts many of the invading species. It is the exotics that thrive in our changing ecosystem.

Current reports on the state of the environment here and around the world may seem dire, but it is not too late for us to work for change. We still have the power to influence the course of events around us. We simply have to decide that **we care about other species**. Humans are not the only species of value on the earth!

Changes in the Florida environment have allowed foreign species to flourish in areas where they do not belong.

If we learn to respect the wildlife in Florida, we may begin to appreciate all of the amazing animals that now call our state home.

Florida's Exotic Problem

According to the Florida Fish and Wildlife Conservation Commission, our state is currently home to 48 known species of exotic reptiles, 4 exotic amphibian species, 155 species of exotic birds, and 31 exotic mammal species. Many other non-native species under observation by state scientists might be breeding in small local populations living in only one or two counties.

Scientists agree that there is an urgent need to reduce the number of exotic animals living and breeding around the state. The first step is to encourage Floridians not to buy exotic animals for pets. The second step is to help exotic pet owners stop abandoning their animals in the wild.

Since 2006, the Florida Fish and Wildlife Conservation Commission has been sponsoring "Nonnative Pet Amnesty Day" events. These events take place on weekends in various cities around the state. Unwanted reptiles, amphibians, fish, birds, and mammals are turned in. The animals are examined by veterinarians, and disease-free pets are placed in new homes. In February 2008, more than 100 south Floridians handed in almost 150 unwanted exotic pets at the Miami Metrozoo.

Programs like this one help to increase public awareness and alter undesirable behaviors. Such changes should help to reduce the number of exotic animals let loose in the state. However, we must still deal with the problem of the millions of exotic animals already living in the wild in Florida.

In Florida, releasing exotic wildlife is a crime, a first-degree misdemeanor subject to a year in prison and a $1000 fine.

My Iguana Friends

My yard is full of iguanas because I live on a tree-lined canal that empties into a lake. On the seawall in my backyard, Common Green Iguanas of all ages and sizes sun themselves. They are sweet, quiet, and calm creatures. They move slowly when they are not bothered. If iguanas were people, I think they would wear pajamas, eat snacks, and watch TV all day!

My iguana friends are used to me. But if you run up to them, they will scoot up a tree or dive into the water faster than you would believe possible. In these instances, the iguana is like an Olympic athlete and impossible to catch. If you corner an iguana, it might whip you with its tail. Or they may scratch or bite you in self-defense. They won't chase you, though, and will not attack you if you are not bothering them.

Some of my human friends have taken in the iguanas I've rescued over the years. Their Green Iguanas use litter boxes, and they will claw at the refrigerator door when they are hungry! You can pet these domesticated iguanas like you would pet a dog or cat.

Not all iguana species are easy to train. Reptiles in general do not make good pets and tend to be unhappy in captivity. They prefer to be outside in the sunlight, where they can forage for natural food and look for mates. Reptiles want to be with their own species, not ours.

Think about this before you select an exotic reptile like an iguana for a pet.

Pet stores sell all kinds of exotic pets that can create problems if they escape or are abandoned in the wild.

It would be impossible to remove all of the non-native animals living and breeding here. Imagine how much it would cost to capture and evict the widespread populations of, for example, Green Iguanas, Cane Toads, Monk Parakeets, Muscovy Ducks, or even feral cats! Using poisons to rid the state of undesirable nuisance animals would damage or kill off native species as well. Wildlife biologists studying the problem of invasive species have yet to come up with a practical solution to this difficult problem.

What You Can Choose to Do

What do you think might be the simplest yet most important contribution you could make to help with Florida's exotic animal problem? Yes, that's right: **Never release your own pet into the wild.**

In fact, it would be extraordinarily helpful if you could **avoid buying an exotic animal for a pet.** You know from reading this book how damaging to the environment non-native species can be. And you are aware of the reasons why wild animals do not make good pets. This information should help you to make the best decision when choosing a pet.

What can you do about all the exotic species living in the parks, lakes, fields, and forests in your part of the state? Well, you can choose to be afraid of these animals. Or you can simply ignore them. Most people do.

But now that you have read this book and learned so much about the various species of non-native animals here in Florida, you may choose instead to become more aware of our wildlife. You may choose to respect the exotic species. In fact, you might even choose to get to know as much as you can about the exotic animals living in your neighborhood. And tell your friends and family about these incredible animals too.

Everglades National Park includes only 25 percent of the original Everglades wetlands.

You can take your camera, binoculars, and a notebook into backyards and backwoods. You can sit quietly by a lake and observe, or hike through a park. Where else in the country can you see South American iguanas, Cuban frogs, African snakes, and rainforest parrots and monkeys—without even going to the zoo? Bring home photos, drawings, and written notes. Show your parents and classmates what you have seen.

Practice safe observation. Use this book to help identify exotic species. You know not to go up to or attempt to capture any exotic animal on the loose. But you can certainly observe the many different species living all around us.

Think about it: Animals want the same things we do in life. Like us, animals look for food and a place to raise their families in peace and safety. Animals are just trying to get through another day on our beautiful, dangerous planet. They have as much right to be here—in our yards, in our state, on our planet—as we do. After all, our world is *their* natural place too.

Exotics have arrived in Florida because humans have brought them here. We have overdeveloped, invaded, kidnapped, and destroyed nature all over the globe. ***Our interventions have changed the face of the planet.***

Most of the plants and animals found around the world can be imported into the U.S. without many—or any—restrictions. Most urban areas and many rural areas are overrun by exotic plants and animals. Obviously, more regulation is required to keep exotic species from so easily entering our state. But laws are difficult to pass, and even more difficult to enforce.

Let's face it: Many of the exotic animal species living in the neighborhoods and parks in Florida are here to stay. And we are the ones who created the new Florida fauna. Now we must take responsibility for the changes we see in our ecosystem.

As humans, we have a tendency to fear changes in our environment. Yet, all around us nature is demonstrating so beautifully the never-ending change that is life here on planet Earth. Why not enjoy the ever-evolving scenery nature provides? Getting to know the wildlife available to us here in the state of Florida may help us discover our true natures. We can learn about our own inner wildness.

There is much to enjoy outdoors in nature. We can find out amazing secrets about life, things we can never learn unless we step beyond our fear of the new and unknown. Armed with the information in this book, you might choose to explore the exotic side of Florida. Perhaps you will learn something quite wonderful about yourself along the way.

References

Ake, Anne. *Everglades: An Ecosystem Facing Choices and Challenges*. Sarasota, Florida: Pineapple Press, 2008.

Alden, Peter, Rick Cech, and Gil Nelson. *National Audubon Society Field Guide to Florida*. New York: Alfred A. Knopf, 1998.

Alsop, Fred J., III. *Birds of Florida*. A Smithsonian Handbook. New York: DK Publishing Inc., 2002.

Badger, David, and John Netherton, photographer. *Lizards: A Natural History of Some Uncommon Creatures–Extraordinary Chameleons, Iguanas, Geckos and More*. St. Paul, Minnesota: Voyageur Press, 2006.

Bartlett, R.D., and Patricia P. Bartlett. *A Field Guide to Florida Reptiles and Amphibians*. Houston, Texas: Gulf Publishers, 1999.

Bittner, Mark. *The Wild Parrots of Telegraph Hill: A Love Story...with Wings*. New York: Three Rivers Press, 2004.

Burger, Joanna. *The Parrot Who Owns Me: The Story of a Relationship*. New York: Random House, 2001.

Carmichael, Peter, and Winston Williams. *Florida's Fabulous Reptiles and Amphibians: Snakes, Lizards, Alligators, Frogs, and Turtles*. Tampa, Florida: World Publications, 1991.

Childs, Craig. *The Animal Dialogues: Uncommon Encounters in the Wild*. New York: Little, Brown and Company, 2007.

Collard, Sneed B. *Alien Invaders: The Continuing Threat of Exotic Species*. London: Franklin Watts, 1996.

Collard, Sneed B. *Science Warriors: The Battle Against Invasive Species*. New York: Houghton Mifflin, 2008.

Cox, George W. *Alien Species in North America and Hawaii: Impacts on Natural Ecosystems*. Washington, D.C.: Island Press, 1999.

Douglas, Marjory Stoneman. *The Everglades: River of Grass*. 60th Anniversary Edition. Sarasota, Florida: Pineapple Press, 2007.

Epps, Susan Allene. *Parrots of South Florida*. Sarasota, Florida: Pineapple Press, 2007.

Gerholt, James E. *Anacondas*. Edina, Minnesota: Abdo, 1996.

Green, Alan, and The Center for Public Integrity. *Animal Underworld: Inside America's Black Market for Rare and Exotic Species*. New York: Public Affairs, 1999.

Guiberson, Brenda. *Exotic Species: Invaders in Paradise*. Twenty-First Century Books, 1999.

Halliday, Tim, and Kraig Adler, editors. *Firefly Encyclopedia of Reptiles and Amphibians*. Buffalo, New York: Firefly Books Ltd., 2002.

Islam, Stephan B. *Anoles: Those Florida Yard Lizards*. Orlando, Florida: Commahawk Publishing, 2006.

Langone, John J. *Our Endangered Earth: Our Fragile Environment and What We Can Do About It.* Boston: Little, Brown and Company, 1992.

Maehr, David S., and Herbert W. Kale II. *Florida's Birds.* Second Edition. Sarasota, Florida: Pineapple Press, 2007.

Mattison, Chris. *The New Encyclopedia of Snakes.* Princeton, New Jersey: Princeton University Press, 2007.

May, Suellen. *Invasive Aquatic and Wetland Animals.* New York: Chelsea House, 2007.

May, Suellen. *Invasive Terrestrial Animals.* New York: Chelsea House, 2006.

McGovern, Bernie. *Florida Almanac 2007–2008.* Gretna, Louisiana: Pelican Publishing Company, 2007.

Meshaka, Walter E., Brian P. Butterfield, and J. Brian Hauge. *The Exotic Amphibians and Reptiles of Florida.* Malabar, Florida: Krieger Publishing Company, 2004.

Mooney, Harold A., and Richard J. Hobbs, editors. *Invasive Species in a Changing World.* Washington, D.C.: Island Press, 2000.

Newton, Michael. *Florida's Unexpected Wildlife: Exotic Species, Living Fossils, and Mythical Beasts in the Sunshine State.* Gainesville, Florida: University Press of Florida, 2007.

Ohr, Tim, editor. *Florida's Fabulous Natural Places.* Tampa, Florida: World Publications, 2003.

Ricciuti, Ed. *The Snake Almanac.* New York: The Lyons Press, 2001.

Townsend, John. *Incredible Reptiles.* Chicago: Raintree Press, 2006.

Whitney, Ellie, D. Bruce Means, and Anne Rudloe. *Priceless Florida: Natural Ecosystems and Native Species.* Sarasota, Florida: Pineapple Press, 2004.

Resources

Animal Rights Foundation of Florida

For information on animal welfare, visit: www.arff.org

Born Free USA

For information on exotic pet abuse, visit: www.bornfreeusa.org

Everglades Cooperative Invasive Species Management Area

To report sightings of invasives in the Everglades, contact: www.evergladescisma.org

Florida Fish and Wildlife Conservation Commission

- For more information about exotic species, visit: www.myfwc.com/WILDLIFE HABITATS/Nonnative_index.htm
- For information on exotic species laws and permits, visit: www.myfwc.com/RULESANDREGS/Rules_Nonnative.htm
- To request the ban of sales of exotic species in Florida, e-mail your letters to: commissioners@myfwc.com
- For a list of wildlife trappers in your area, visit: www.myfwc.com/License/Permits_NuisWild.htm
- To report python sightings, call: 1-888-483-4681 (python hotline)
- To report exotic species sightings, call: 1-888-404-3922 (wildlife hotline)
- To report alligators or caimans, call: 1-866-392-4286 (Nuisance Alligator hotline)
- To report exotic fish sightings, send photos and descriptions to: fishcoll@myfwc.com

IguanaInvasion.com

For more information on exotic species in Florida, visit: www.iguanainvasion.com

National Park Service

To learn about educational programs such as "Intruders in Paradise," "Don't Let it Loose," and "Project Wild," visit: www.nps.gov/ever/naturescience/learnandteach.htm

National Wildlife Federation

To learn more about threatened wildlife, visit: www.nwf.org

Nature Conservancy

To learn more about invasives, visit: www.nature.org/initiatives/invasivespecies

Southeastern Outdoors

For a list of wildlife rehabilitation facilities, visit: www.southeasternoutdoors.com/wildlife/rehabilitators/index-rehabilitators.html

Tampa Bay Estuary Program

For an educational program on invasive animals and plants, visit: www.tbep.org/isteachersguide/index.html

United States Department of Agriculture

To visit the National Invasive Species Information Center, go to: www.invasivespeciesinfo.gov

U.S. Fish and Wildlife Service

To see the endangered species listing, visit: www.fws.gov/endangered

Educator's Resources

Sunshine State Standards

For Standards that address exotic animals and the environment, visit: www.floridastandards.org

This book can be used to address various benchmarks in the Sunshine State Standards, such as "SC.912.L.17.8: Recognize the consequences of the losses of biodiversity due to catastrophic events, climate changes, human activity, and the introduction of invasive, non-native species."

Educator's Guide

For classroom ideas and homework activities designed for integration into science coursework, visit: www.iguanainvasion.com/students_teachers.html

Glossary

bacteria: simple one-celled organisms that can be helpful or harmful to humans and animals; some cause disease and/or produce toxins that cause illness

barrier island: a piece of land that lies between the coastline and the sea, protecting beach and coastal habitat from erosion and storms

brood: a group of young birds hatched together and cared for by one mother

burrow: a hole or tunnel dug in the ground for nesting

chameleons: various species of color-changing lizards from the family Chamaeleontidae; not native to North America

clutch: a set of eggs incubated at one time by a mother bird or reptile

coral reef: limestone formation created by millions of tiny sea animals; found mostly in the warm, shallow waters of the South Pacific Ocean, the Indian Ocean, and the Caribbean Sea, as well as along the Florida coast

ecosystem: a complex organization in nature made up of a living community (animals, humans) and its environment (soil, water, temperature and climate, air, nutrients, and energy)

endangered species: animals and plants threatened with extinction

erode: to wear away; beach erosion is often caused by overdevelopment

euthanize: to end a life painlessly, typically with the injection of a lethal drug

Everglades: wetlands extending from Lake Okeechobee to the Florida Bay and the Gulf of Mexico; includes the 1.5 million–acre Everglades National Park in the southwestern tip of the state

fauna: animals, especially the group of animals living in a particular region

fungus: any organism that belongs to the kingdom Fungi, including yeasts, molds, and mushrooms

generalist: a species that is not specifically adapted to a particular environment; one that is not specialized, which means it is not limited to certain foods or habitats

global warming: an increase in the average temperature of the Earth's surface; influenced by human activities, especially the burning of fossil fuels (coal, oil, and natural gas) and the clearing of land for building and farming

habitat: the area or type of environment in which a species lives by itself or in a community

hatchling: a newly hatched bird, reptile, amphibian, or fish

hybrid species: offspring produced by breeding animals of two different species

incubate: to keep eggs warm enough to allow for proper development until hatching

juvenile: a young animal that is not yet sexually mature

mammals: warm-blooded vertebrate animals that have hair and produce milk for their young; include humans and other species

mangroves: more than 100 species of high-rooted trees and bushes that grow in brackish water in coastal habitats; protect land from erosion and storms

marine: native to or living in the sea

metabolism: the combined processes of the body that maintain life and produce energy

migratory birds: those species which move from one region and settle in another, usually seasonally

neuter: to surgically alter an animal so that it is not able to reproduce

newts: small salamanders with bright coloring that live on land and breed in the water

nocturnal: most active at night

non-marine: not of the sea; a land animal

non-migratory birds: species which do not move from region to region on a regular or seasonal basis

non-venomous: not poisonous; animals may bite but will not transmit toxins

pesticide: chemicals used to kill insects, weeds, fungi, and rodents; organisms develop resistance to pesticides over time, and the harmful effects of these poisons are contributing to environmental damage throughout the world

plague: a type of bacteria carried by rodents such as rats, squirrels, and prairie dogs; fleas infected with the bacteria can transfer the disease from pets to humans, causing serious illness

predator: an animal that lives by preying on other animals

prey: an animal that is hunted by another animal for food

primates: mammals that have highly developed hands and feet with fingers, toes, and thumbs capable of grasping; include humans and the animals that most resemble them (apes, monkeys, and others)

Quakers: members of a Christian faith from England called the Society of Friends who once wore stiff, biblike collars

reclutch: to lay a new set of eggs (for instance, after a nest is invaded)

rodents: small gnawing mammals with sharp upper teeth; include rats, mice, squirrels, and prairie dogs

salamanders: small, lizardlike amphibians with four undeveloped, weak legs

salmonella: harmful bacteria that cause food poisoning, typhoid, and other infectious diseases in humans and animals

spay: to surgically alter a female animal so that she can no longer reproduce

specialist: a species which is only suited for life in a specific environment due to food preferences, temperature needs, or other habitat requirements; does not have the survival advantages of generalized species

territorial: indicating the desire to live in and defend a specific area of habitat

terrapins: turtle species that live in brackish water, which is a mix of fresh and salt water

threatened species: plant or animal at risk for becoming endangered

tortoises: land turtles with high, rounded shells

toxin: a poison that can cause disease when introduced into body tissues

tranquilizer: a drug used to soothe, calm, or bring on a state of unconsciousness

troop: a group of monkeys

venom: a poison transmitted by a bite or sting from a snake, spider, or other venomous animal

venomous: able to transmit venom

vertebrates: animals having a backbone or spine; include mammals, birds, reptiles, amphibians, and fish

virus: a microscopic parasite that must live on or in another organism; may cause illness in the host organism

Acknowledgments

Our thanks to:

Adam Stern and the Miami Metrozoo

Carla at the Zoological Society of Florida

Gary Morse, Scott Harden, and the Florida Fish and Wildlife Conservation Commission

Michael Oster at www.LaptopNoise.com

Joe Kegley at www.WildlifeSouth.com

Jeanne Brodsky and everyone at Strictly Reptiles

John Welch and the Okeeheelee Nature Center

Professor Arnold Arluke at Northeastern University

Rey Becerra at Billie's Swamp Safari

Verid and Virginia at the Folke Peterson Wildlife Center

Dana Denson, Florida Department of Environmental Protection

Photo Credits

Photos were taken by Virginia Aronson unless otherwise noted.

Frontispiece, middle: Photo by Mel Goss

Frontispiece, bottom: Photo by Mel Goss

Page 2, middle: Photo by Adam G. Stern

Page 2, right: Photo by Michael Oster

Page 6: Photo by Adam G. Stern

Page 7: Photo by Michael Oster

Page 11: Photo by Mel Goss

Page 13: Photo by Mel Goss

Page 14, top: Photo by Adam G. Stern

Page 14, bottom: Photo courtesy of Okeeheelee Nature Center

Page 15: Photo by Adam G. Stern

Page 18, bottom: Photo by Arnold Arluke

Page 23: Photo of Adam G. Stern courtesy of Janeen A. Feiger

Page 25, bottom: Photo by Adam G. Stern

Page 26, top: Photo by Adam G. Stern

Page 26, bottom: Photo by Mel Goss

Page 28: Photo by Mel Goss

Page 30: Photo by Adam G. Stern

Page 31, top: Photo by Adam G. Stern

Page 33: Photo by Adam G. Stern

Page 35: Photos courtesy of Dana Denson, Florida Department of Environmental Protection

Page 36, top: Photo by Adam G. Stern

Page 36, bottom: Photo by Mel Goss

Page 37: Photo by Mel Goss

Page 40: Photo by Arnold Arluke

Page 41: Photo by Mel Goss

Page 44, top: Photo by Joseph C. Kegley

Page 44, bottom: Photo by Adam G. Stern

Page 45: Photo by Joseph C. Kegley

Page 49, top: Photo by Joshua Lutz

Page 49, bottom: Photo by Arnold Arluke

Page 50: Photo by Adam G. Stern

Page 51: Photo courtesy of USDA

Page 54: Photo by Mel Goss

Page 55, bottom: Photo by Mel Goss

Page 56: Photos by Mel Goss

Page 58: Photo by Mel Goss

Page 69: Author photos by Arnold Arluke

Index

Photos are indicated by **boldface** type.

About the Authors

Allyn Szejko is a licensed humane trapper and a licensed wildlife rehabilitator. She is the recipient of numerous awards for her work, including the 2001 Animal Kindness Award, which recognizes citizens who make notable voluntary contributions to animal welfare. She has also been honored by the South Florida Eco Award committee. Allyn has written and starred in two educational videos about coexisting with Florida wildlife developed by the Folke H. Peterson Foundation. Both films have been shown on educational television and are available in Florida schools and libraries. She often speaks at schools and is involved in Florida politics pertaining to animal rights and protection of the environment. Allyn lives in Boca Raton with her family.

Virginia Aronson is the author or co-author of 30 books. She has published nutrition textbooks for students, medical guides and biographies for young readers, and health books for all ages. Virginia is the author of two other Pineapple Press titles for young readers: *Konnichiwa Florida Moon* and *Gift of the Unicorn*, both biographies of environmental leaders in the state of Florida. She lives in south Florida with her family.

Visit the authors at www.IguanaInvasion.com.

Here are some other books from Pineapple Press on related topics. For a complete catalog, write to Pineapple Press, P.O. Box 3889, Sarasota, Florida 34230-3889, or call (800) 746-3275. Or visit our web-site at www.pineapplepress.com.

Also by Virginia Aronson
Gift of the Unicorn: The Story of the Lue Gim Gong, Florida's Citrus Wizard by Virginia Aronson. Lue Gim Gong came to Florida from China as a boy. He overcame poverty and discrimination to become a brilliant horticulturist who blessed the world with his gift. (hb)

Konnichiwa Florida Moon: The Story of George Morkiami, Pineapple Pioneer by Virginia Aronson. This is the inspirational story of George Morikami, one of the earliest Japanese Americans to settle in Florida. (hb)

Young Readers
The Young Naturalist's Guide to Florida, Second Edition, by Peggy Sias Lantz and Wendy A. Hale. This enticing book shows you where and how to look for Florida's most interesting natural features and creatures. Take it along on your next walk in the woods. (pb)

Drawing Florida's Wildlife by Frank Lohan. The clearest, easiest method yet for learning to draw Florida's birds, reptiles, amphibians, and mammals. (pb)

Everglades: An Ecosystem Facing Choices and Challenges by Anne E. Ake. The Everglades is like no other place in the world. Its shallow, slowly flowing waters create an ecosystem of mysterious beauty with a great diversity of plant and animal life. But the Everglades ecosystem is in trouble. Learn about what's being done to help, and why the Everglades are worth saving. (hb)

The Gopher Tortoise by Patricia Sawyer Ashton and Ray E. Ashton Jr. Color photos and easy text make clear the behavior and daily life of the gopher tortoise. Find out how scientists study these unique animals and try to protect them from human encroachment on their habitat. (hb, pb)

Dinosaurs of the South by Judy Cutchins and Ginny Johnston. Dinosaurs lived in the southeastern United States. Loaded with full-color fossil photos as well as art to show what dinosaurs might have looked like. (hb)

Ice Age Giants of the South by Judy Cutchins and Ginny Johnston. Learn about the huge animals and reptiles that lived here during the Ice Age. Meet saber-toothed cats, dire wolves, mammoths, giant sloths, and more. (hb)

Giant Predators of the Ancient Seas by Judy Cutchins and Ginny Johnston. Meet the giant creatures that prowled the waters of prehistory. (hb)

My Florida Facts by Russell W. Johnson and Annie P. Johnson. Learn facts about Florida—from the state capital to the number of counties in Florida and much more—through the catchy lyrics of the song "My Florida Facts." Includes CD. (hb)

Adults
Stalking the Plumed Serpent by D. Bruce Means. The author, an expert on the eastern diamondback rattlesnake, reveals the biological complexity and beauty of animals that he has studied. Most people loathe these reptiles and amphibians, but Means shows his love for creatures that go bump in the night. (hb)

Everglades: River of Grass, 60th Anniversary Edition, by Marjory Stoneman Douglas with an update by Michael Grunwald. Before 1947, when Marjory Stoneman Douglas named the Everglades a "river of grass," most people considered the area worthless. She brought the world's attention to the need to preserve the Everglades. In the Afterword, Michael Grunwald tells us what has happened since then. (hb)

Priceless Florida by Ellie Whitney, D. Bruce Means, and Anne Rudloe. An extensive guide (432 pages, 800 color photos) to the incomparable ecological riches of this unique region, presented in a way that will appeal to young and old, laypersons and scientists. Complete with maps, charts, species lists. (hb, pb)